Math Expressions

Volume 2

**Developed by
The Children's Math Worlds Research Project**

PROJECT DIRECTOR AND AUTHOR
Dr. Karen C. Fuson

This material is based upon work supported by the
National Science Foundation
under Grant Numbers
ESI-9816320, REC-9806020, and RED-935373.

Any opinions, findings, and conclusions, or recommendations expressed in this material
are those of the author and do not necessarily reflect the views of the National Science Foundation.

 HOUGHTON MIFFLIN HARCOURT

Teacher Reviewers

Kindergarten
Patricia Stroh Sugiyama
Wilmette, Illinois

Barbara Wahle
Evanston, Illinois

Grade 1
Sandra Budson
Newton, Massachusetts

Janet Pecci
Chicago, Illinois

Megan Rees
Chicago, Illinois

Grade 2
Molly Dunn
Danvers, Massachusetts

Agnes Lesnick
Hillside, Illinois

Rita Soto
Chicago, Illinois

Grade 3
Jane Curran
Honesdale, Pennsylvania

Sandra Tucker
Chicago, Illinois

Grade 4
Sara Stoneberg Llibre
Chicago, Illinois

Sheri Roedel
Chicago, Illinois

Grade 5
Todd Atler
Chicago, Illinois

Leah Barry
Norfolk, Massachusetts

Special Thanks

Special thanks to the many teachers, students, parents, principals, writers, researchers, and work-study students who participated in the Children's Math Worlds Research Project over the years.

Credits

Cover art: (t) © Charles Cormany/Workbook Stock/Jupiter Images, (b) Noah Strycker/Shutterstock

Ilustrative art: Robin Boyer/Deborah Wolfe, LTD; Dave Clegg, Spatial Graphics, Tim Johnson
Technical art: Nesbitt Graphics, Inc.
Photos: Nesbitt Graphics, Inc.; Page 309 © Anna Clopet/Corbis

2011 Edition
Copyright © 2009 by Houghton Mifflin Harcourt Publishing Company

ISBN: 978-0-547-47375-8

1 2 3 4 5 6 7 8 9 10   1421   19 18 17 16 15 14 13 12 11 10

4500228408   X B C D E

VOLUME 2 CONTENTS

Continued ▶

Mini Unit 10 Shapes and Patterns

Unit 11 3-Digit Addition and Subtraction

Understanding Numbers to 1,000

Money Through $10.00

Adding to 1,000

3-Digit Subtraction

3-Digit Addition and Subtraction

* This lesson consists only of activities from the Teacher Edition.

Mini Unit 12 Metric Measurement and 3-D Shapes

Unit 13 Multiplication and Fractions

Groups and Arrays

Shares, Symmetry, and Fractions

The Nature of Chance

Continued ▶

* This lesson consists only of activities from the Teacher Edition.

Mini Unit 14 Non-Standard and Standard Units of Measure

Extension Lessons

Glossary

Class Activity

▶ **Name Quadrilaterals**

Vocabulary

square   parallelogram
rectangle   quadrilateral

	Is it a **square**? Explain.	Is it a **rectangle**? Explain.	Is it a **parallelogram**? Explain.	Is it a **quadrilateral**? Explain.
1.	Yes. It has 4 equal sides and the corners are square.			
2.				
3.				
4.				

Class Activity

Name _____

▶ **Draw Diagonals**

> A line segment that connects opposite corners of a quadrilateral is called a **diagonal**.

5. Draw a diagonal in this square.

6. What shapes are formed by drawing a diagonal in a square?

   _____

7. What are your observations about the two shapes that are formed?

   _____

   _____

8. Draw a diagonal in this rectangle.

9. What shapes are formed by drawing a diagonal in a rectangle?

   _____

Diagonals of Quadrilaterals

Dear Family,

Your child is working on a geometry unit about dividing quadrilaterals into smaller shapes by drawing diagonals and line segments that connect the midpoints of opposite sides. The main goal of this unit is to help children develop their spatial abilities.

Diagonals are line segments that join opposite corners of a quadrilateral.

A midpoint divides a line segment into two equal parts.

When you join the midpoints of opposite sides, you divide a quadrilateral into four parts.

Encourage your child to look for quadrilaterals in your home and neighborhood. Ask your child to predict what shapes will be formed by drawing diagonals in the quadrilaterals or by connecting the midpoints of opposite sides.

For example, ask your child to describe the shape of a sandwich before you cut it. Ask your child to then predict what shapes will be formed if you cut the sandwich along the diagonals or along the line segments made by joining the midpoints on opposite sides.

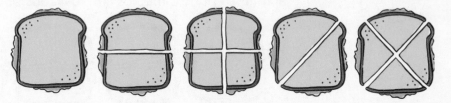

In this unit, your child will be asked to draw diagonals on three identical shapes. Your child will draw a different diagonal in each of the first two shapes and draw both diagonals in the third shape.

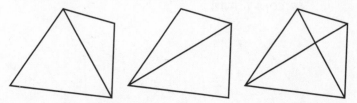

If you have any questions or comments, please call or write to me.

Sincerely,
Your child's teacher

Estimada familia:

Su niño está trabajando en una unidad de geometría. Aprenderá a dividir cuadriláteros en figuras más pequeñas dibujando diagonales y segmentos que unen los puntos medios de lados opuestos. El objetivo principal de esta unidad es ayudar a los niños a desarrollar su sentido espacial.

Las diagonales son segmentos que unen vértices opuestos de un cuadrilátero.

Los puntos medios dividen un segmento en dos partes iguales.

A •————————•————————• B

Cuando se unen los puntos medios de lados opuestos se divide el cuadrilátero en cuatro partes.

Anime a su niño a buscar cuadriláteros en la casa y en el vecindario. Pídale que prediga qué figuras se formarán al dibujar diagonales en los cuadriláteros o al unir los puntos medios de lados opuestos.

Por ejemplo, pida a su niño que describa la figura de un sándwich antes de cortarlo. Pídale que prediga qué figuras se formarán is corta el sándwich por las diagonales o por los segmentos formados al unir los puntos medios con los lados opuestos.

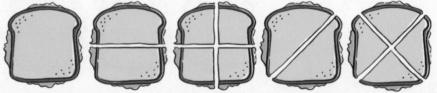

En esta unidad su niño deberá dibujar diagonales en tres figuras idénticas. Se le pedirá que dibuje una diagonal diferente en cada una de las primeras dos figuras y que dibuje ambas diagonales en la tercera figura.

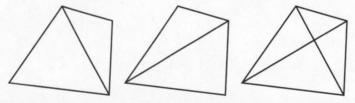

Si tiene alguna pregunta o comentario, por favor comuníquese conmigo.

Atentamente,
El maestro de su niño

Diagonals of Quadrilaterals

Class Activity

Name _____

▶ Explore Methods of Finding Midpoints

The **midpoint** of a line segment divides the line segment into two equal parts.

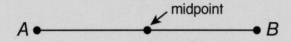

Use at least two different ways to find the midpoint of each line segment and draw a dot at that point.

1. J •————————• K

2. C •————• D

3. E •————————————• F

4. P •————————————————• Q

5. **Explain Your Thinking** Describe two of the ways you used to find the midpoints of the line segments above.

_____

_____

_____

_____

_____

_____

Class Activity

Vocabulary

opposite sides

▶ **Connect Midpoints**

6. Mark the midpoints of two **opposite sides**.

7. What shapes do you think you will see when you connect the midpoints?

_____

8. Connect the midpoints. Describe the shapes you see.

_____

9. Mark the midpoints of the other two opposite sides.

10. Connect the midpoints. What shapes do you see?

_____

11. How are these shapes like the shapes in the first square? How are they different?

_____

_____

Class Activity

▶ **Add Line Segments to Shapes**

Draw one diagonal.	Draw the other diagonal.	Draw both diagonals.
1.		
2.		
3.		
4.		

Class Activity

▶ **Add Line Segments to Shapes**

Use estimation to find the midpoints.

Connect the midpoints of two opposite sides.	Connect the midpoints of the other two sides.	Draw both line segments.
5.		
6.		
7.		
8.		

Practice with Diagonals and Connecting Midpoints

Draw one diagonal.	Draw the other diagonal.	Draw both diagonals.
1.		
2.		

3. Find the midpoint of the line segment and draw a dot at that point.

H •————————————————————————• I

Name _____

4. Draw one diagonal in the square.

Describe the new shapes.

_____

_____

5. Draw two diagonals in the parallelogram.

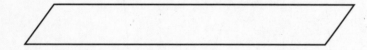

Describe the new shapes.

_____

_____

6. Draw two diagonals in this quadrilateral.

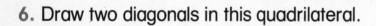

Describe the new shapes.

_____

_____

Test

7. Connect the midpoints of two opposite sides.

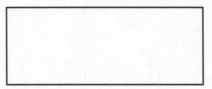

Describe the new shapes.

_____

_____

8. Connect the midpoints of two opposite sides. Then connect the midpoints of the other two sides.

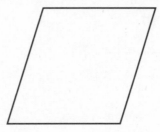

Describe the new shapes.

_____

_____

9. Connect the midpoints of two opposite sides. Then connect the midpoints of the other two sides.

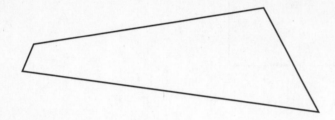

Describe the new shapes.

_____

_____

10. **Extended Response** Use two different methods to find the midpoint of this line segment.

S •————————————————• T

Describe both methods.

_____

_____

_____

_____

_____

_____

_____

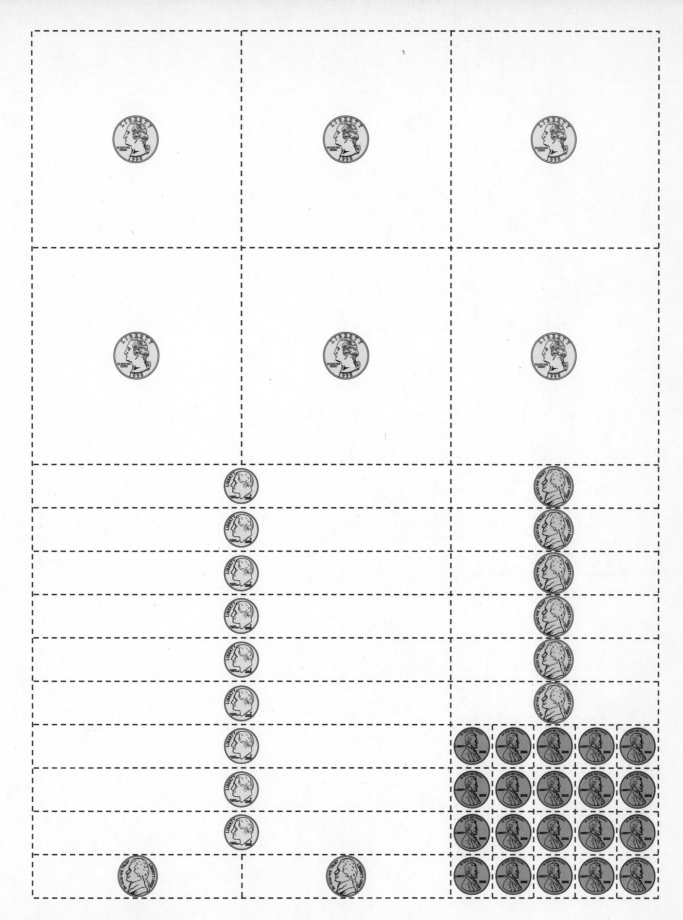

Cut on dashed lines.

Coin Cards

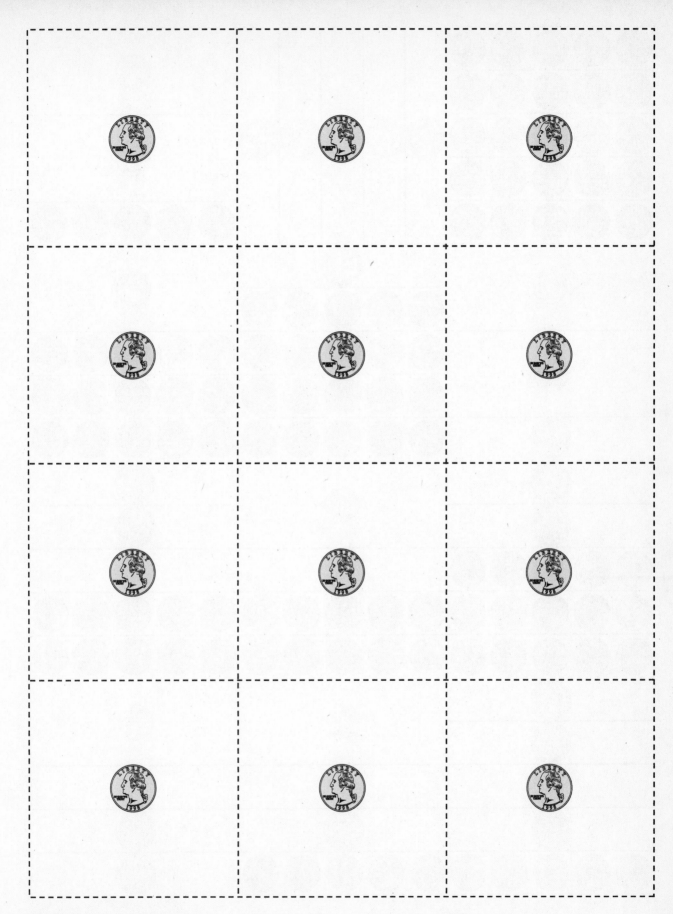

Cut on dashed lines.

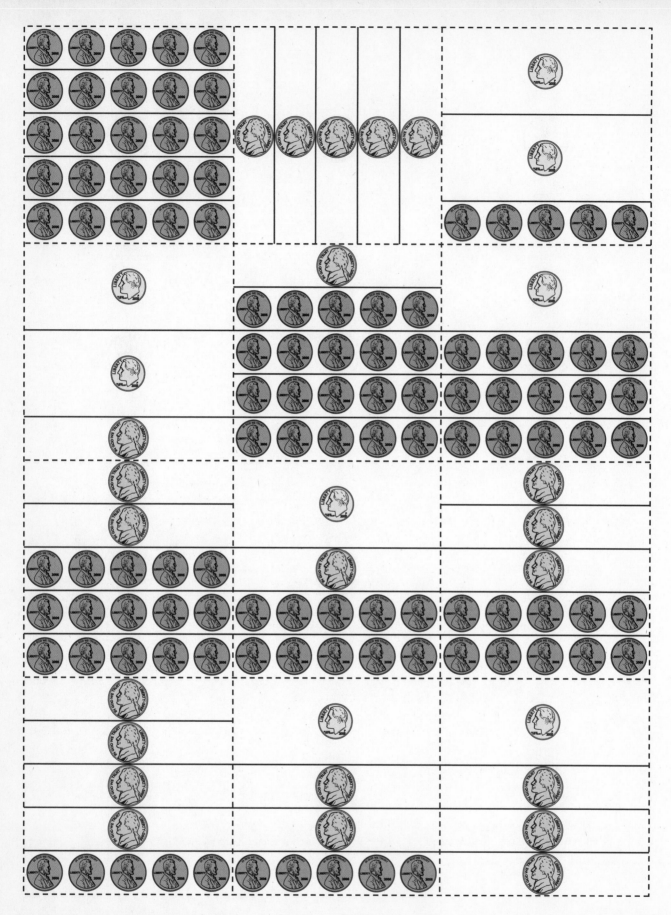

Cut only on dashed lines.

Quarter Squares (back)

Dear Family,

In this unit, your child will explore and count coins and various coin combinations. Children will also explore dollars and combine different coins to equal one dollar.

25¢   +   25¢   +   10¢   +   10¢   +   10¢   +   10¢   +   10¢   =   100¢

Then your child will count both dollars and coins.

Say: $1.00 $1.25 $1.35 $1.40

You can help at home by providing opportunities for your child to practice counting money. Begin with amounts less than $1.00.

Please call if you have any questions or concerns. Thank you for helping your child to learn mathematics.

Sincerely,
Your child's teacher

Carta a la familia

Estimada familia:

En esta unidad su niño va a contar monedas y diversas combinaciones de monedas. Los niños también trabajarán con dólares y combinarán diferentes monedas para igualar el valor de un dólar.

25¢ + 25¢ + 10¢ + 10¢ + 10¢ + 10¢ + 10¢ =   100¢

Luego su niño contará tanto billetes de dólares como monedas.

Se dice: $1.00 $1.25 $1.35 $1.40

Usted puede ayudar en su casa ofreciéndole al niño oportunidades de practicar contando dinero. Empiece con cantidades menores que $1.00.

Si tiene alguna duda o comentario, por favor comuníquese conmigo. Gracias por ayudar a su niño a aprender matemáticas.

Atentamente,
El maestro de su niño

Explore Quarters

Cut on dashed lines.

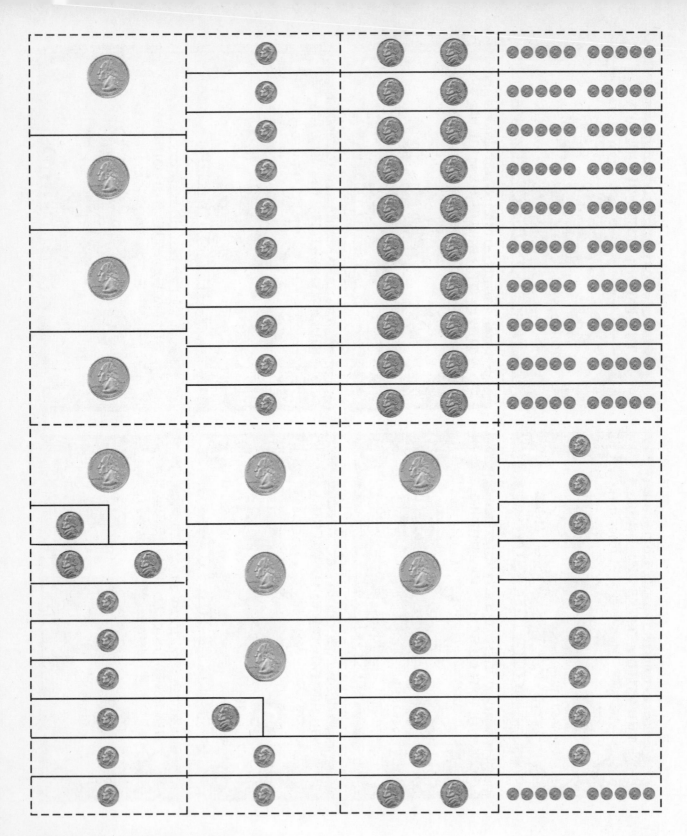

Cut only on dashed lines.

Dollar Equivalents (back)

Class Activity

▶ **Problems Using 100-Partners**

When you subtract, you can use the following drawings
to help you ungroup.

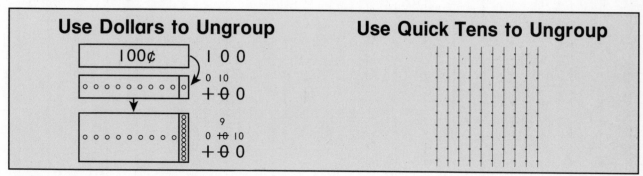

Use Dollars to Ungroup **Use Quick Tens to Ungroup**

Solve the story problems.

1. The baker baked 100 loaves of
   bread. He sold 73 loaves. How
   many loaves are left?

   _____
   label

2. I had 100 flowers in my garden. I
   gave 26 of them away. How many
   flowers are left in my garden?

   _____
   label

3. The letter carrier had 100 letters in
   his bag. He delivered 52 letters.
   How many letters are left in his bag?

   _____
   label

4. **On the Back** Use the drawings to help you solve the
   exercises your teacher gives you.

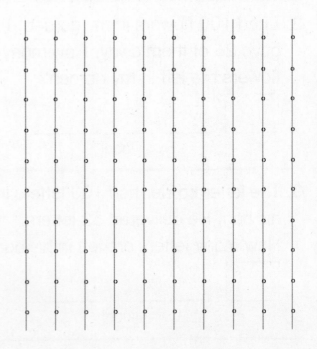

Partners and Subtraction

Dive the Deep

$11 - 6 = \boxed{5}$ $12 - \boxed{6} = 6$ $13 - 8 = \boxed{5}$

$12 - 7 = \boxed{5}$ $17 - \boxed{8} = 9$ $15 - 6 = \boxed{9}$

$12 - 9 = \boxed{3}$ $13 - \boxed{5} = 8$ $11 - 9 = \boxed{2}$

$13 - 4 = \boxed{9}$ $14 - \boxed{6} = 8$ $13 - 9 = \boxed{4}$

$11 - 5 = \boxed{6}$ $17 - \boxed{9} = 8$ $15 - 7 = \boxed{8}$

$14 - 9 = \boxed{5}$ $11 - \boxed{8} = 3$ $14 - 8 = \boxed{6}$

$14 - 7 = \boxed{7}$ $12 - \boxed{4} = 8$ $12 - 5 = \boxed{7}$

$16 - 7 = \boxed{9}$ $16 - \boxed{8} = 8$ $11 - 3 = \boxed{8}$

$11 - 7 = \boxed{4}$ $15 - \boxed{7} = 8$ $13 - 6 = \boxed{7}$

$12 - 3 = \boxed{9}$ $16 - \boxed{9} = 7$ $18 - 9 = \boxed{9}$

$13 - 7 = \boxed{6}$ $11 - \boxed{4} = 7$ $12 - 8 = \boxed{4}$

Dive the Deep

$11 - 5 = \boxed{6}$ $\qquad$ $12 - \boxed{6} = 6$ $\qquad$ $13 - 5 = \boxed{8}$

$12 - 5 = \boxed{7}$ $\qquad$ $17 - \boxed{9} = 8$ $\qquad$ $15 - 9 = \boxed{6}$

$12 - 3 = \boxed{9}$ $\qquad$ $13 - \boxed{8} = 5$ $\qquad$ $11 - 2 = \boxed{9}$

$13 - 9 = \boxed{4}$ $\qquad$ $14 - \boxed{8} = 6$ $\qquad$ $13 - 4 = \boxed{9}$

$11 - 6 = \boxed{5}$ $\qquad$ $17 - \boxed{8} = 9$ $\qquad$ $15 - 8 = \boxed{7}$

$14 - 5 = \boxed{9}$ $\qquad$ $11 - \boxed{3} = 8$ $\qquad$ $14 - 6 = \boxed{8}$

$14 - 7 = \boxed{7}$ $\qquad$ $12 - \boxed{8} = 4$ $\qquad$ $12 - 7 = \boxed{5}$

$16 - 9 = \boxed{7}$ $\qquad$ $16 - \boxed{8} = 8$ $\qquad$ $11 - 8 = \boxed{3}$

$11 - 4 = \boxed{7}$ $\qquad$ $15 - \boxed{8} = 7$ $\qquad$ $13 - 7 = \boxed{6}$

$12 - 9 = \boxed{3}$ $\qquad$ $16 - \boxed{7} = 9$ $\qquad$ $18 - 9 = \boxed{9}$

$13 - 6 = \boxed{7}$ $\qquad$ $11 - \boxed{7} = 4$ $\qquad$ $12 - 4 = \boxed{8}$

Dive the Deep

Name _____

Class Activity

▶ Explain the **Expanded Method**

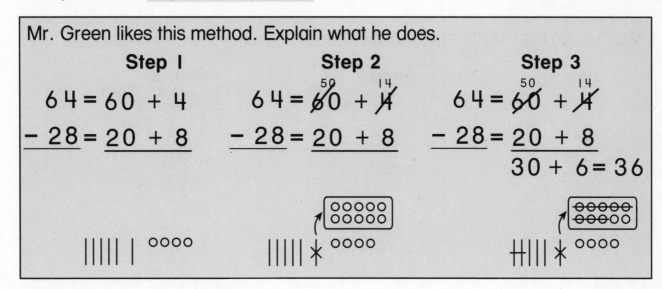

Mr. Green likes this method. Explain what he does.

Step 1	**Step 2**	**Step 3**

Step 1:
$$64 = 60 + 4$$
$$-28 = \underline{20 + 8}$$

Step 2:
$$64 = \overset{50}{\cancel{6}}0 + \overset{14}{\cancel{4}}$$
$$-28 = \underline{20 + 8}$$

Step 3:
$$64 = \overset{50}{\cancel{6}}0 + \overset{14}{\cancel{4}}$$
$$-28 = \underline{20 + 8}$$
$$30 + 6 = 36$$

▶ Try the Expanded Method

Show your work numerically and with a Proof Drawing.

1. $$\begin{array}{r} 42 \\ -19 \\ \hline \end{array}$$

2. $$\begin{array}{r} 75 \\ -46 \\ \hline \end{array}$$

3. $$\begin{array}{r} 81 \\ -37 \\ \hline \end{array}$$

Class Activity

Name _____

Vocabulary

Ungroup First Method

▶ **Explain the Ungroup First Method**

Mrs. Green likes this method. Explain what she does.

Step 1	Step 2	Step 3
64 − 28	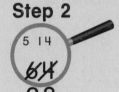5 14 6̸4̸ − 28	5 14 6̸4̸ − 28 ___ 36

▶ **Try the Ungroup First Method**

Show your work numerically and with a Proof Drawing.

4. 42
   − 19

5. 75
   − 46

6. 81
   − 37

Two Methods of Subtraction

Dear Family,

Your child is now learning how to subtract 2-digit numbers. The big mystery is how to get enough ones in order to subtract. As with addition, children first use methods they invent themselves. We have found that children take pride in using their own methods.

In this program, children learn two methods for 2-digit subtraction, but children may use any method that they understand, can explain, and can do fairly quickly.

Expanded Method	Ungroup First Method
Step 1 "Expand" each number to show that it is made up of tens and ones.	**Step 1** Check to see if there are enough ones to subtract from. If not, ungroup by opening up 1 of the 6 tens in 64 to be 10 ones. 4 ones plus these new 10 ones make 14 ones. We draw a "magnifying glass" around the top number to focus children on whether they need to ungroup before subtraction.

Expanded Method

Step 1 "Expand" each number to show that it is made up of tens and ones.

$$64 = 60 + 4$$
$$-28 = 20 + 8$$

Step 2 Check to see if there are enough ones to subtract from. If not, ungroup a ten into 10 ones and add it to the existing ones.

$$\overset{50\ +\ 14}{64 = 60 + 4}$$
$$-28 = 20 + 8$$

Step 3 Subtract to find the answer. Children may subtract from left to right or right to left.

$$\overset{50\ +\ 14}{64 = 60 + 4}$$
$$-28 = 20 + 8$$
$$30 + 6 = 36$$

Ungroup First Method

Step 1 Check to see if there are enough ones to subtract from. If not, ungroup by opening up 1 of the 6 tens in 64 to be 10 ones. 4 ones plus these new 10 ones make 14 ones. We draw a "magnifying glass" around the top number to focus children on whether they need to ungroup before subtraction.

Step 2 Subtract to find the answer. Children may subtract from left to right or right to left.

In explaining any method they use, children are expected to use "tens and ones" language. This shows that they understand they are subtracting 2 tens from 5 tens (not 2 from 5) and 8 ones from 14 ones.

Please call if you have any questions or comments.

Sincerely,
Your child's teacher

Carta a la familia

Estimada familia:

Su niño está aprendiendo a restar números de 2 dígitos. El misterio es cómo obtener suficientes unidades para poder restar. como en la suma, los niños primero usan métodos que ellos mismos inventan. Hemos notado que los niños se sienten orgullosos de usar sus propios métodos.

En este programa, los niños aprenden dos métodos para la resta con números de 2 dígitos, pero pueden usar cualquier método que comprendan, puedan explicar y puedan hacer relativamente rápido.

Método extendido	Método de desagrupar primero
Paso 1 "Extender" cada número para mostrar que consta de decenas y unidades.	**Paso 1** Observar si hay suficientes unidades para restar. Si no las hay, entonces desagrupar duna de las 6 decenas en 64 para obtener 10 unidades. 4 unidades más las 10 unidades nuevas hacen 14 unidades. Dibujamos una "lupa" alrededor del número superior para que los niños piensen si necesitan desagrupar antes de restar.

$$64 = 60 + 4$$
$$-28 = 20 + 8$$

Paso 2 Observar si hay suficientes unidades para restar. Si no las hay, desagrupar una decena para formar 10 unidades y sumarla a las unidades existentes.

$$\overset{50\ +\ 14}{64 = 6\!\!\!/0 + \!\!\!/4}$$
$$-28 = 20 + 8$$

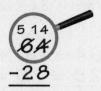

Paso 2 Restar para hallar la respuesta. Los niños pueden restar de izquierda a derecha o de derecha a izquierda.

Paso 3 Restar para hallar la respuesta. Los niños pueden restar de izquierda a derecha o de derecha a izquierda.

$$\overset{50\ +\ 14}{64 = 6\!\!\!/0 + \!\!\!/4}$$
$$-28 = 20 + 8$$
$$30 + 6 = 36$$

Cuando los niños explican el método que usan, deben usar un lenguaje relacionado con "decenas y unidades". Esto demuestra que comprenden que están restando 2 decenas de 5 decenas (no 2 de 5) y 8 unidades de 14 unidades.

Si tiene alguna duda o comentario, por favor comuníquese conmigo.

Atentamente,
El maestro de su niño

Class Activity

Name _____

▶ **Solve and Discuss**

Subtract.

1.   7 5
    $\underline{-\ 4\ 7}$

2.   5 4
    $\underline{-\ 1\ 8}$

3.   9 4
    $\underline{-\ 3\ 6}$

4.   6 6
    $\underline{-\ 3\ 4}$

5.   8 5
    $\underline{-\ 5\ 8}$

6.   8 9
    $\underline{-\ 6\ 9}$

7.   8 2
    $\underline{-\ 5\ 9}$

8.   9 7
    $\underline{-\ 7\ 8}$

9.   6 5
    $\underline{-\ 2\ 8}$

10.   7 8
    $\underline{-\ 1\ 9}$

11.   5 3
    $\underline{-\ 2\ 6}$

12.   9 1
    $\underline{-\ 4\ 6}$

Going Further

▶ **Introduce Estimating Differences**

Vocabulary

estimate
difference

Estimate the **difference**.

$$78 - 42$$

You can use number lines and rounding to estimate a difference.

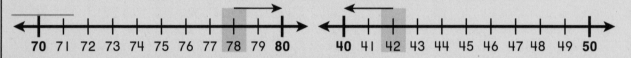

78 is closer to 80 than 70. Round up to 80.

42 is closer to 40 than 50. Round down to 40.

$$80 - 40 = 40$$

▶ **Practice Estimating Differences**

Round each number to the nearest ten. Estimate the difference.

1. $67 - 43$

   _____ − _____ = _____

2. $72 - 58$

   _____ − _____ = _____

3. $87 - 52$

   _____ − _____ = _____

4. $61 - 49$

   _____ − _____ = _____

5. There were 74 plants in Mr. Codero's greenhouse.
   Then Mr. Codero sold 37 plants. About how many
   plants did Mr. Codero have in his greenhouse then?
   Estimate to find the answer.

   _____

6. **Write Your Own** On a separate sheet of paper,
   write a subtraction story problem that can be solved
   by using an estimate.

Practice and Explain a Method

Vocabulary

Expanded Method
Ungroup First Method

▶ **Explain Ungrouping 200**

Explain why 200 = 100 + 90 + 10.

▶ **Explain the Expanded Method**

Explain how ungrouping and subtraction work.
Relate steps here to steps in the drawing above.

Expanded Method

$$
\begin{array}{r}
200 \\
-\ 68
\end{array}
=
\begin{array}{r}
\cancel{200}^{100} + \cancel{100}^{90} \overset{+\ 10}{} + 0 \\
60 + 8 \\
\hline
100 + 30 + 2 = 132
\end{array}
\quad \text{or} \quad
\cancel{200}^{100} + \overset{90}{0} + \overset{+\ 10}{0}
$$

▶ **Explain the Ungroup First Method**

Explain how ungrouping and subtraction work.
Relate steps here to steps in the drawing above.

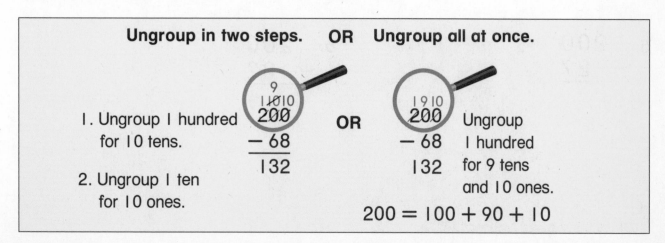

Ungroup in two steps.   OR   **Ungroup all at once.**

1. Ungroup 1 hundred for 10 tens.

2. Ungroup 1 ten for 10 ones.

$$
\begin{array}{r}
\overset{9}{\cancel{200}}{}^{\,1\!\cancel{0}10} \\
-\ 68 \\
\hline
132
\end{array}
$$

OR

$$
\begin{array}{r}
\overset{1\ 9\ 10}{\cancel{200}} \\
-\ 68 \\
\hline
132
\end{array}
$$

Ungroup 1 hundred for 9 tens and 10 ones.

200 = 100 + 90 + 10

Class Activity

► **Practice Both Methods**

Use the Ungroup First Method or the Expanded Method
to find each difference.

1. $\begin{array}{r} 200 \\ -87 \\ \hline \end{array}$

2. $\begin{array}{r} 200 \\ -89 \\ \hline \end{array}$

3. $\begin{array}{r} 200 \\ -46 \\ \hline \end{array}$

4. $\begin{array}{r} 200 \\ -38 \\ \hline \end{array}$

5. $\begin{array}{r} 200 \\ -27 \\ \hline \end{array}$

6. $\begin{array}{r} 200 \\ -82 \\ \hline \end{array}$

Name _____

▶ **Subtraction Sprint**

7 – 4 =	10 – 6 =	17 – 9 =
13 – 5 =	15 – 9 =	6 – 4 =
9 – 3 =	11 – 3 =	10 – 7 =
11 – 2 =	18 – 9 =	13 – 9 =
8 – 6 =	8 – 4 =	12 – 5 =
12 – 9 =	9 – 7 =	16 – 8 =
6 – 3 =	13 – 6 =	14 – 7 =
15 – 7 =	12 – 3 =	10 – 6 =
10 – 8 =	16 – 7 =	8 – 5 =
8 – 3 =	7 – 5 =	11 – 9 =
14 – 5 =	12 – 4 =	13 – 7 =
11 – 7 =	17 – 8 =	14 – 8 =
10 – 4 =	9 – 4 =	10 – 5 =
12 – 8 =	14 – 8 =	12 – 6 =
16 – 9 =	11 – 4 =	15 – 7 =
14 – 6 =	9 – 6 =	13 – 6 =
9 – 5 =	12 – 7 =	11 – 8 =
13 – 9 =	14 – 9 =	12 – 3 =
10 – 3 =	13 – 4 =	13 – 5 =
15 – 8 =	7 – 3 =	15 – 6 =
11 – 5 =	11 – 6 =	13 – 8 =

Name _____

Class Activity

▶ Decide When to Ungroup

Decide if you need to ungroup. Then subtract.

1. 134
  − 78

Did you ungroup a ten to get more ones? _____

Did you ungroup a hundred to get more tens? _____

2. 134
  − 73

Did you ungroup a ten to get more ones? _____

Did you ungroup a hundred to get more tens? _____

3. 158
  − 37

Did you ungroup a ten to get more ones? _____

Did you ungroup a hundred to get more tens? _____

4. 158
  − 39

Did you ungroup a ten to get more ones? _____

Did you ungroup a hundred to get more tens? _____

5. 146
  − 57

Did you ungroup a ten to get more ones? _____

Did you ungroup a hundred to get more tens? _____

6. 146
  − 35

Did you ungroup a ten to get more ones? _____

Did you ungroup a hundred to get more tens? _____

Practice with the Ungrouping First Method

Name _____

▶ Subtract with Zeroes

Decide if you need to ungroup. Then subtract.

1.
```
  108
-  46
```

2.
```
  103
-  65
```

3.
```
  150
-  79
```

4.
```
  102
-  83
```

5.
```
  160
-  92
```

6.
```
  107
-  61
```

7.
```
  106
-  38
```

8.
```
  170
-  40
```

9.
```
  180
-  93
```

10.
```
  140
-  57
```

11.
```
  150
-  84
```

12.
```
  106
-  43
```

Class Activity

Name _____

▶ **Solve and Discuss**

Decide if you need to ungroup. Then subtract.

13.
```
  I 0 6
-   8 I
```

14.
```
  I I 0
-   I 8
```

15.
```
  I 9 0
-   7 2
```

16.
```
  I 0 7
-   3 8
```

17.
```
  I 3 0
-   2 2
```

18.
```
  I 2 0
-   6 3
```

Solve each story problem. Make a
math drawing if you need more help.

Show your work.

19. Larry sells cars. He wants to sell
109 cars this month. So far he has
sold 34. How many more cars
does he need to sell?

label

20. Abbie grilled I I0 burgers for the
school picnic. 79 were eaten. How
many are left?

label

Zero in the Ones or Tens Place

Class Activity

Name _____

▶ **Use Exact Change**

First, see how much money you have. Then decide what to buy. Pay for the item with **exact change**. Then write how much money you have left.

Yard Sale

Cork Board	Toy Rabbit	Toy Guitar	Perfume	Knit Cap
78¢	84¢	75¢	89¢	99¢

1. I have 162¢ in my pocket.

I bought the _____.

$$\begin{array}{r} 1\ 6\ 2¢ \\ -\ ¢ \\ \hline \end{array}$$

I have _____ ¢ left.

2. I have 143¢ in my pocket.

I bought the _____.

$$\begin{array}{r} 1\ 4\ 3¢ \\ -\ ¢ \\ \hline \end{array}$$

I have _____ ¢ left.

3. I have 154¢ in my pocket.

I bought the _____.

$$\begin{array}{r} 1\ 5\ 4¢ \\ -\ ¢ \\ \hline \end{array}$$

I have _____ ¢ left.

4. I have 126¢ in my pocket.

I bought the _____.

$$\begin{array}{r} 1\ 2\ 6¢ \\ -\ ¢ \\ \hline \end{array}$$

I have _____ ¢ left.

Model Subtraction with Money **295**

Going Further

Name _____

▶ **Use Decimal Notation for Money**

Write the money amount.

1. 134¢ = __1__ dollar __3__ dimes __4__ pennies = $ __1__.__3__ __4__

2. 76¢ = _____ dollar _____ dimes _____ pennies = $ _____._____ _____

3. 179¢ = _____ dollar _____ dimes _____ pennies = $ _____._____ _____

4. 58¢ = _____ dollar _____ dimes _____ pennies = $ _____._____ _____

Find the difference. Use play money to help you ungroup, if you wish.

5.
```
$ 1 . 4 4
-   . 2 3
```

6.
```
$ 1 . 2 5
-   . 9 5
```

7.
```
$ 1 . 6 3
-   . 9 5
```

8.
```
$ 1 . 5 8
-   . 4 5
```

9.
```
$ 1 . 3 6
-   . 7 5
```

10.
```
$ 1 . 9 2
-   . 9 5
```

Model Subtraction with Money

Class Activity

▶ Addition and Subtraction Story Problems

Draw a Math Mountain to solve each story problem. Show how you add or subtract.

Show your work.

1. Teresa had 85 blocks. Then she found 47 more under the couch. How many blocks does Teresa have now?

   [ ] _____

   label

2. Krina's class made 163 masks. They hung 96 of them in the library. How many masks do they have left?

   [ ] _____

   label

3. Andy's plant was 138 inches tall. It grew 27 inches. How many inches tall is his plant now?

   [ ] _____

   label

4. The school store had 144 glue sticks. They sold 79 so far this year. How many glue sticks do they have left?

   [ ] _____

   label

Going Further

► Estimate to Find the Answer

Use any method to **estimate** the solutions to
exercises 1–4. Write the estimate on the line.
Then use the estimate to help you match the
exercise to its answer.

1.

_____

$$\begin{array}{r} 92 \\ -\ 17 \end{array}$$ •

• 9

2.

_____

$$\begin{array}{r} 72 \\ +\ 52 \end{array}$$ •

• 93

3.

_____

$$\begin{array}{r} 33 \\ 22 \\ +\ 38 \end{array}$$ •

• 124

4.

_____

$$\begin{array}{r} 48 \\ -\ 39 \end{array}$$ •

• 75

Jason has 38 cartoon videos and 19 movie videos.
He wants to buy a cabinet that will hold 70 videos.

5. About how many videos does he have in all? _____

6. Will they all fit in the cabinet? _____

Story Problems with Addition and Subtraction

Class Activity

▶ **Find Equations for Math Mountains**

1. Write all of the equations for 83, 59, and 24.

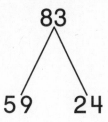

$59 + 24 = 83$ $83 = 59 + 24$

_____   _____

_____   _____

2. Write all of the equations for 142, 96, and 46.

$96 + 46 = 142$ $142 = 96 + 46$

_____   _____

_____   _____

3. **On the Back** Show how you can subtract to find the unknown partner for $96 + \boxed{} = 142$.

Math Mountain Equations with Larger Numbers

Class Activity

► Practice Preferred Methods

Add or subtract. Watch the sign!

1.
$$\begin{array}{r} 1\,5\,1 \\ -\ \ 6\,3 \\ \hline \end{array}$$

2.
$$\begin{array}{r} 4\,6 \\ +\ 7\,2 \\ \hline \end{array}$$

3.
$$\begin{array}{r} 1\,0\,5 \\ -\ \ 7\,4 \\ \hline \end{array}$$

4.
$$\begin{array}{r} 9\,7 \\ +\ 8\,8 \\ \hline \end{array}$$

5.
$$\begin{array}{r} 6\,4 \\ -\ 2\,3 \\ \hline \end{array}$$

6.
$$\begin{array}{r} 7\,3 \\ +\ 6\,6 \\ \hline \end{array}$$

7.
$$\begin{array}{r} 1\,8\,0 \\ -\ \ 5\,6 \\ \hline \end{array}$$

8.
$$\begin{array}{r} 9\,4 \\ +\ 3\,8 \\ \hline \end{array}$$

9.
$$\begin{array}{r} 1\,4\,7 \\ -\ \ 8\,9 \\ \hline \end{array}$$

10.
$$\begin{array}{r} 4\,3 \\ +\ 6\,7 \\ \hline \end{array}$$

11.
$$\begin{array}{r} 1\,7\,6 \\ -\ \ 7\,8 \\ \hline \end{array}$$

12.
$$\begin{array}{r} 8\,3 \\ +\ 7\,9 \\ \hline \end{array}$$

13. **On the Back** Explain each step you do to subtract
63 from 155. Use tens and ones language.

Practice Addition and Subtraction **301**

Practice Addition and Subtraction

Name _____

► **Introduce the Juice Bar**

Grapefruit Juice 68¢	Red Apple Juice 59¢	Lemon Juice 77¢	Pear Juice 78¢
Green Apple Juice 89¢	Peach Juice 88¢	Orange Juice 97¢	Cantaloupe Juice 87¢
Pineapple Juice 98¢	Raspberry Juice 65¢	Banana Juice 76¢	Watermelon Juice 56¢
Grape Juice 67¢	Celery Juice 58¢	Tomato Juice 96¢	Carrot Juice 79¢

Class Activity

Name _____

▶ Continue Buying and Selling

Choose two juices from the Juice Bar you would like to mix together. Find the total cost. Then find the change from two dollars.

1. I pick _____

   and _____.

   Juice #1 price: _____ ¢

   Juice #2 price: **+** _____ ¢

         Total: _____

   200¢ − _____ = _____

   My change is _____ ¢.

2. I pick _____

   and _____.

   Juice #1 price: _____ ¢

   Juice #2 price: **+** _____ ¢

         Total: _____

   200¢ − _____ = _____

   My change is _____ ¢.

3. I pick _____

   and _____.

   Juice #1 price: _____ ¢

   Juice #2 price: **+** _____ ¢

         Total: _____

   200¢ − _____ = _____

   My change is _____ ¢.

4. I pick _____

   and _____.

   Juice #1 price: _____ ¢

   Juice #2 price: **+** _____ ¢

         Total: _____

   200¢ − _____ = _____

   My change is _____ ¢.

Buy and Sell with Two Dollars

Class Activity

▶ **Practice the Adding Up Method**

Add up to solve each story problem.

Show your work.

1. Doug has 92 baseball cards. After he goes shopping today, he will have 175 baseball cards. How many baseball cards is Doug going to buy?

☐ _____
   label

2. Myra had 87 dollars. After she bought some gifts, she had 68 dollars. How much money did Myra spend on gifts?

☐ _____
   label

3. There were 151 tons of corn in a silo in May. In June there were 213 tons of corn. How many tons of corn were added to the silo?

☐ _____
   label

4. Azim found 113 golf balls. After he gave some of them to Max, he had 54 golf balls left. How many golf balls did Azim give to Max?

☐ _____
   label

Going Further

Name _____

▶ **Choose a Reasonable Answer**

Each picture shows an item Ella wants to buy and
the amount of money she has. Circle the most
reasonable estimate of how much more money
Ella needs to buy the item.

1.

    80¢

3¢

30¢

300¢

3,000¢

2.

121¢

20¢

40¢

60¢

80¢

3.

159¢

8¢

80¢

800¢

8,000¢

4.

WATER 109¢

1¢

10¢

100¢

1,000¢

Story Problems with Unknown Partners

Class Activity

Name _____

► Practice the Adding Up Method

Solve each story problem.   **Show your work.**

1. Justin read 162 comics. Trina read
   93 comics. How many more comics
   did Justin read than Trina?

   [ ] _____
        label

2. Maya made 64 drawings. Philip
   made 132 drawings. How many
   fewer drawings did Maya make
   than Philip?

   [ ] _____
        label

3. There were 187 birds in the zoo.
   The zoo received some more birds,
   and now they have 246 birds. How
   many birds did the zoo receive?

   [ ] _____
        label

4. Rita had 121 pens. She gave some
   pens to her friends. Now she has
   75 pens. How many pens did Rita
   give away?

   [ ] _____
        label

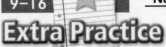

9-16

Extra Practice

Name _____

▶ **Alphabet Math Puzzle**

Add or subtract. Then, solve the alphabet puzzle by
using the answer for the exercise to find the next
letter in the puzzle.

A = 42
    + 79

O = 142
    − 17

H = 137
    − 76

M = 125
    + 38

C = 126
    − 84

N = 121
    − 37

D = 84
    + 58

A = 163
    − 75

T = 88
    + 49

I ___ ___ ___ ___ ___ ___ ___ ___ ___ ___ !
   42 121 84 142 125 163 88 137 61

More Story Problems with Unknown Partners

Class Activity

▶ **Math and Science**

Dr. Grant is a zoologist who studies how animals move. She collects data to use in her reports.

One data table tells how far some animals can move in 1 second.

Distance Moved in 1 Second

Animal	Cheetah	Chicken	Elephant	Lion	Spider
Distance	103 feet	13 feet	37 feet	73 feet	1 foot

Dr. Grant wants to compare these distances in a report.
Decide whether a statement is *true* or *not true* or has *no data*.
Ring your answer.

1. An elephant goes farther in 1 second than a lion.

   True   Not True   No Data

2. A cheetah goes farther in 1 second than a spider.

   True   Not True   No Data

3. A chicken and a cheetah travel the same distance in 1 second.

   True   Not True   No Data

4. A spider goes farther in 1 second than a snail.

   True   Not True   No Data

5. Use the data. Write 2 true statements for the report.

   _____

   _____

   _____

Class Activity

Name _____ **Date** _____

▶ **True or False?**

Mathematicians must support their statements with proof. One example can prove that a statement is false. It is harder to show that a statement is true.

Decide whether each statement is true or false. Then show why. Find 3 examples to support true statements. Find one example to show that a statement is false.

1. If you double any number, the answer is always even.

   _____

   _____

2. You can always divide a rectangle into 4 triangles with 1 straight line.

   _____

3. If you add two odd numbers, the total will always be an odd number.

   _____

4. There are many different ways to make 50¢ with nickels, dimes, and quarters.

   _____

   _____

5. Write a math statement. It can be true or false. Tell whether it is true or false. Use examples.

   _____

   _____

   _____

Use Mathematical Processes

Name _____

Count the money.

1.

    25¢   50¢   75¢   85¢   _____ _____ _____ _____

2.

_____ _____ _____ _____ _____ _____ _____ _____ _____

3.

_____ _____ _____ _____ _____ _____ _____ _____ _____

Subtract. Ungroup if you need to.

4.
```
   6 3
 - 2 7
```

5.
```
   8 4
 - 1 9
```

6.
```
   9 2
 - 4 6
```

7.
```
   5 7
 - 2 5
```

Subtract.

8. $\begin{array}{r} 100 \\ -\ \ 18 \\ \hline \end{array}$

9. $\begin{array}{r} 200 \\ -\ \ 43 \\ \hline \end{array}$

10. $\begin{array}{r} 179 \\ -\ \ 81 \\ \hline \end{array}$

11. $\begin{array}{r} 198 \\ -\ \ 56 \\ \hline \end{array}$

12. $\begin{array}{r} 130 \\ -\ \ 67 \\ \hline \end{array}$

13. $\begin{array}{r} 104 \\ -\ \ 13 \\ \hline \end{array}$

14. $\begin{array}{r} 156 \\ -\ \ 39 \\ \hline \end{array}$

15. $\begin{array}{r} 143 \\ -\ \ 84 \\ \hline \end{array}$

Unit Test

Name _____

Solve the story problems.   **Show your work.**

---

16. Vince has 89 purple bicycles and 47 red bicycles in his store. How many bicycles does he have altogether?

    ┌─────────────┐
    │   │ _____
    └─────────────┘   label

---

17. Bonita had 97 raisins. She ate 58 of them. How many raisins are left?

    ┌─────────────┐
    │   │ _____
    └─────────────┘   label

---

18. There are 42 birds at the feeder in our tree. There are 35 more at the feeder on the fence. How many birds are at both feeders in all?

    ┌─────────────┐
    │   │ _____
    └─────────────┘   label

---

19. Jeffrey bought 200 paper cups for his party. 79 cups were used. How many paper cups does Jeffrey have left?

    ┌─────────────┐
    │   │ _____
    └─────────────┘   label

20. Extended Response Explain all the steps you do to subtract 59 from 148.

_____

_____

_____

_____

_____

_____

Class Activity

Name _____

Vocabulary

congruent

▶ Congruent Figures

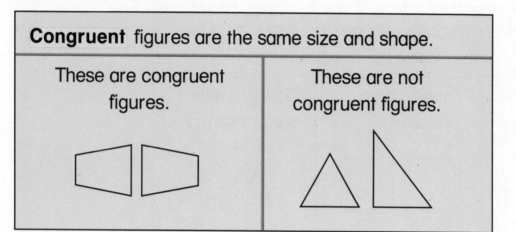

Congruent figures are the same size and shape.

These are congruent figures.	These are not congruent figures.

Which two figures are congruent?

1. Figures _____ and _____ are congruent.

2. Figures _____ and _____ are congruent.

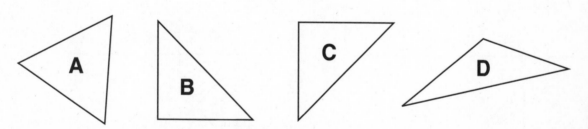

3. Figures _____ and _____ are congruent.

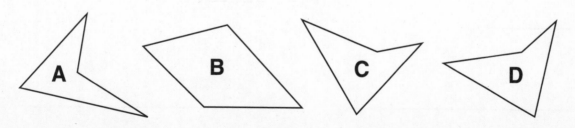

Class Activity

Vocabulary
similar

▶ Similar Figures

Similar figures are the same shape. They may also be the same size, but they don't have to be.

These figures are similar.	These figures are similar.	These figures are not similar.

Are the two figures similar? Write *similar* or *not similar.*

4.

_____

5.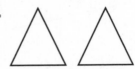

_____

6.

_____

7.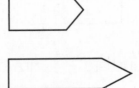

_____

Compare Shapes

► **Sort Figures**

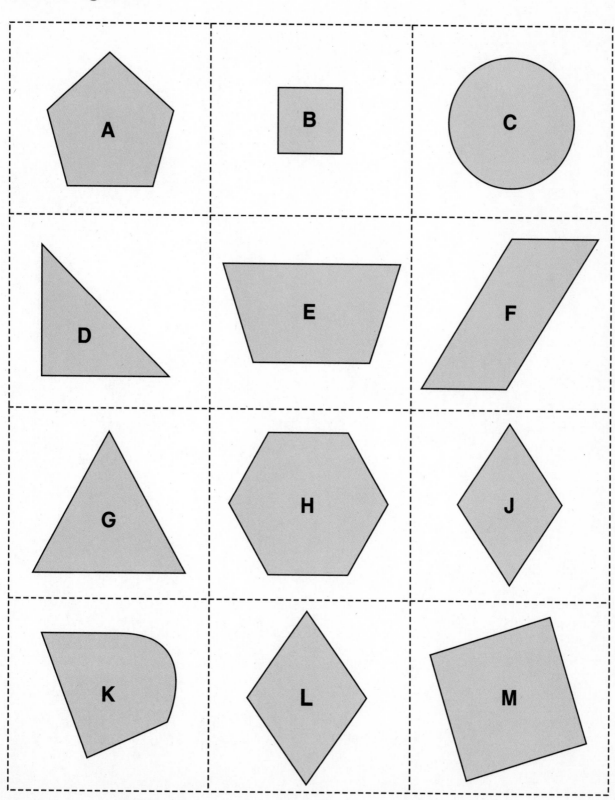

Compare Shapes

Dear Family,

Your child is working on a geometry unit about congruent figures: figures that are the same size and shape. The unit also covers similar figures: figures that are the same shape but not necessarily the same size.

Your child will be sliding figures up, down, left, and right; flipping figures over horizontal and vertical lines; and turning figures around a point.

He or she will also explore different types of patterns, including repeating patterns, growing patterns, and motion patterns (slides, flips, and turns).

Your child will be asked to find the area of figures in square centimeters by counting the number of squares on centimeter-grid paper that a figure covers.

You can help reinforce your child's math learning at home.

• Encourage your child to work on jigsaw puzzles to practice sliding, flipping, and turning figures.

• Have your child find the area of tiled floors in square units by counting square tiles.

• Help your child identify patterns in fabrics, nature, music, and art.

• Create patterns using objects like buttons, paper clips, or coins. Ask your child to continue the pattern. Or you can remove one piece from the pattern and ask your child to identify the missing piece.

If you have any questions or comments, please call or write to me.

Sincerely,
Your child's teacher

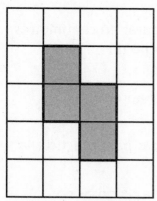

Area of shaded figure =
4 square centimeters

Estimada familia:

Su niño está trabajando en una unidad de geometría sobre figuras congruentes: figuras que tienen el mismo tamaño y forma. La unidad también incluye figuras semejantes: figuras que tienen la misma forma pero no necesariamente el mismo tamaño.

Su niño trasladará figuras hacia arriba, hacia abajo, hacia la izquierda y hacia la derecha; invertirá figuras sobre rectas horizontales y verticales y hará girar figuras alrededor de un punto.

También explorará diferentes tipos de patrones, incluidos patrones que se repiten, patrones que aumentan y patrones de movimiento (traslaciones, inversiones y giros).

Se le pedirá a su niño que halle el área de figuras en centímetros cuadrados contando el número de cuadrados de un papel cuadriculado que están cubiertos por una figura.

Usted puede ayudar a que su niño refuerce el aprendizaje de matemáticas en casa.

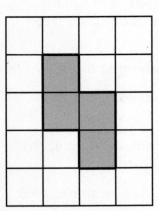

Área de la figura sombreada = 4 centímetros cuadrados

- Anime a su niño a trabajar con rompecabezas para practicar la traslación, la inversión y el giro de figuras.

- Pídale a su niño que halle el área de pisos de baldosas en unidades cuadradas, contando baldosas cuadradas.

- Ayude a su niño a identificar patrones en las telas, la naturaleza, la música y el arte.

- Haga patrones utilizando objetos como botones, sujetapapeles o monedas. Pida a su niño que continúe el patrón. También, puede quitar una pieza del patrón y pedirle al niño que identifique la pieza que falta.

Si tiene alguna pregunta o comentario, por favor comuníquese conmigo.

Atentamente,
El maestro de su niño

Compare Shapes

Vocabulary

combine

Cut out each shape.

Combine shapes.

Combine and Cut Shapes

Cut out each shape.

Cut apart shapes.

Class Activity

▶ Identify Slides

You can **slide** a figure right or left along a straight line.

You can slide a figure up or down along a straight line.

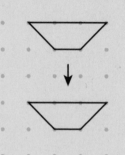

Does each picture show a slide? Write *yes* or *no*.

1.

_____

2.

_____

3.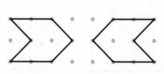

_____

4.

_____

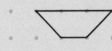

Class Activity

Name _____

▶ Identify Flips

You can **flip** a figure over a **horizontal line**.

You can flip a figure over a **vertical line**.

Does each picture show a flip over the line? Write *yes* or *no*.

5.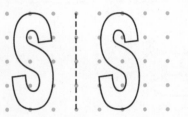

_____

6.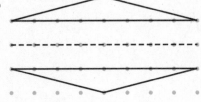

_____

7.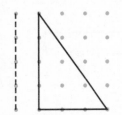

_____

8.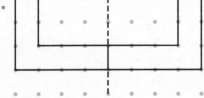

_____

Motion Geometry

▶ **Identify Turns**

You can **turn** or **rotate** a figure around a point.

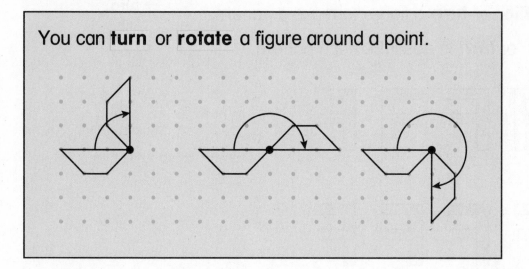

Does each picture show a turn around the point?
Write *yes* or *no*.

9.

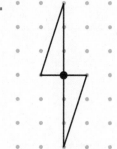

10.

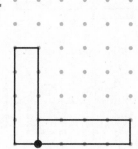

11.

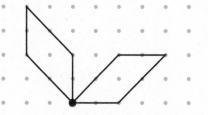

12.

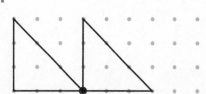

Class Activity

Name _____

Vocabulary
slide
flip
turn

▶ Identify Slides, Flips, and Turns

You can **slide, flip,** or **turn** a figure to make a pattern.

Write *slide, flip,* or *turn* to describe each pattern.

13.

_____

14.

_____

15.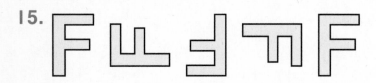

_____

16.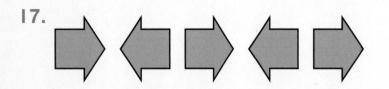

_____

17.

_____

18.

_____

Motion Geometry

Class Activity

► **Extend Patterns**

Draw the next figure in the pattern.

19.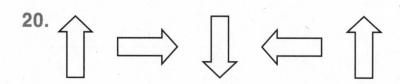

_____

20.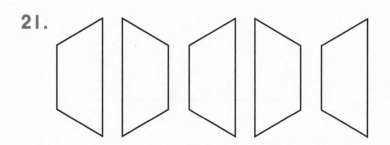

_____

21.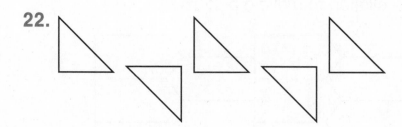

_____

22.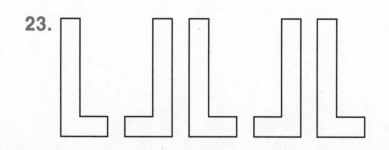

_____

23.

_____

Going Further

Vocabulary

tessellation

▶ **Explore Tessellations**

A **tessellation** is a pattern made by congruent polygons that fit together exactly to cover a surface.

A tessellation is like a tiling pattern that covers a floor.

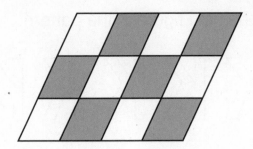

1. Use your ruler to continue the pattern to make a tessellation of triangles.

   Color the triangles to make a pattern.

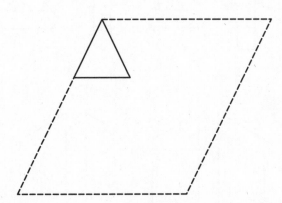

2. Use your ruler to draw more figures to extend this tessellation. Color the tessellation to make a pattern.

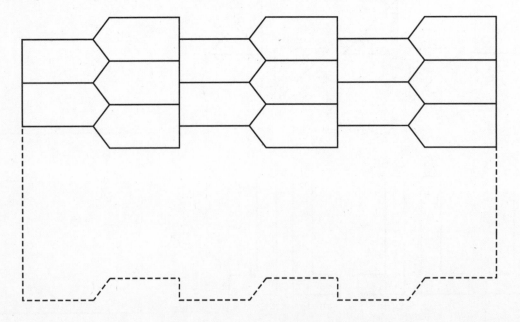

Say each pattern aloud.
Draw what comes next.

1.  _____

2.  _____

3.  _____

Draw what comes next in each **growing pattern**.

4.  _____

5.

 _____

6.

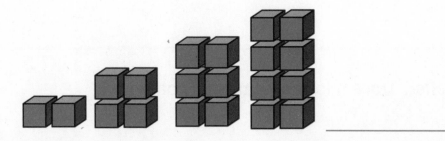 _____

Class Activity

Name _____

Vocabulary

motion pattern

Draw what comes next in each **motion pattern**.

1. ⇨ ⬇ ⇦ ⬆ ⇨ ⬇ ⇦ ⬆ ⇨ ⬇ ⇦ ⬆ ⇨ ⬇ ⇦ ⬆ _____

2.

_____

3. Trace a square by an edge of the grid.

Move it and trace it 4 times.

· · · · · · · · · ·

· · · · · · · · · ·

· · · · · · · · · ·

· · · · · · · · · ·

· · · · · · · · · ·

· · · · · · · · · ·

· · · · · · · · · ·

· · · · · · · · · ·

· · · · · · · · · ·

4. Draw and cut out a letter. Trace it to show a motion pattern.

Patterns with Shapes

Class Activity

Name

Vocabulary
area
square units

▶ Count Square Units

Cover each figure with **square units** and count them to find the **area**.

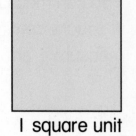

1 square unit

1.

Area = ☐ square units

2.

Area = ☐ square units

3.

Area = ☐ square units

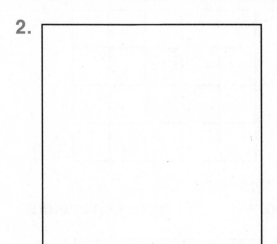

Class Activity

Name _____

Vocabulary

square centimeter

▶ Count Square Centimeters

You can measure area in **square centimeters**.
A square centimeter is a square with sides that
measure 1 cm.

1 square centimeter

Count the number of squares in each shaded figure to
find the area in square centimeters.

4.

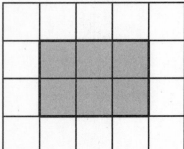

Area = _____ square centimeters

5.

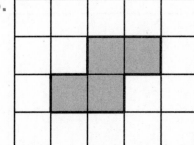

Area = _____ square centimeters

6.

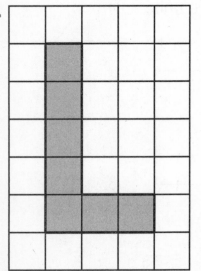

Area = _____ square centimeters

7.

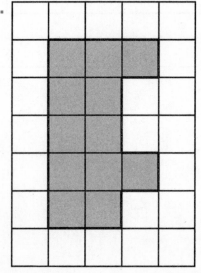

Area = _____ square centimeters

Count Square Units

Name _____

1. Which two shapes are congruent?

Shapes _____ and _____ are congruent.

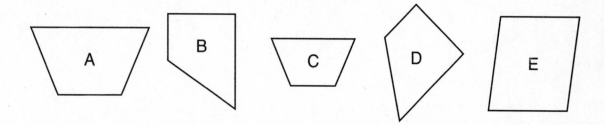

2. Are the two shapes similar? Write similar or not similar.

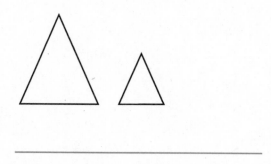

_____

3. Sort these shapes using the rule: quadrilaterals and not quadrilaterals. Write the letters.

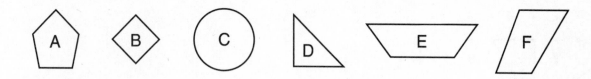

The shapes _____ are quadrilaterals.

The shapes _____ are not quadrilaterals.

4. Does the picture show a slide?
Write yes or no.

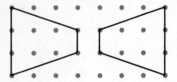

_____

5. Does the picture show a flip over the line?
Write yes or no.

_____

6. Does the picture show a turn around the point?
Write yes or no.

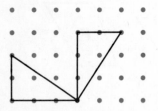

_____

Test

7. Draw the next figure in the pattern.

_____

Find the area in square centimeters.

8.

Area = _____ square centimeters

9.

Area = _____ square centimeters

Name _____

10. **Extended Response** Choose a sorting rule to sort
the shapes into two groups.

My sorting rule is: _____

The shapes _____ are _____.

The shapes _____ are _____.

► Count to 1,000 by Hundreds

Cut on dashed lines.

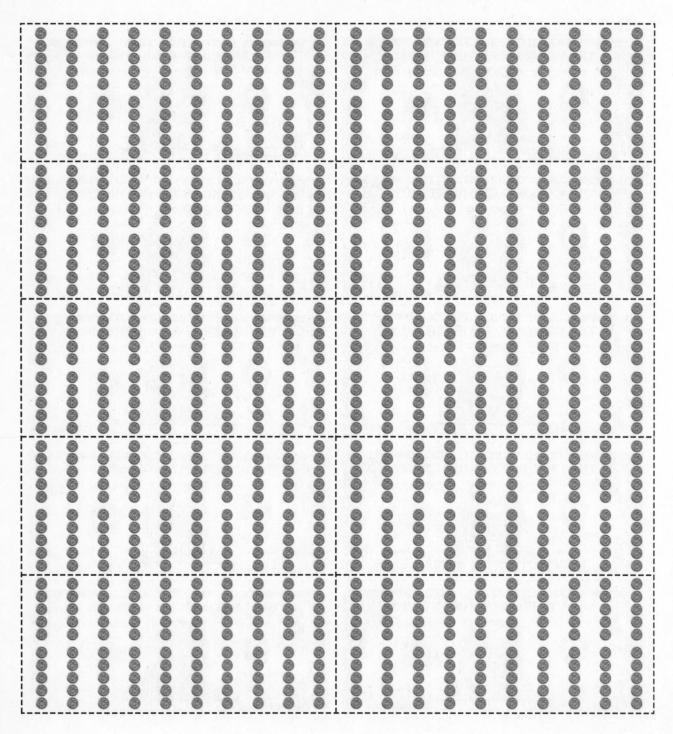

Dollars with Penny Array (back)

Dear Family,

In this unit, children will learn different ways to add 3-digit numbers that have totals less than 1,000, with and without regrouping. One way that children will add 3-digit numbers is by counting to 1,000 by tens and by hundreds.

Count to 1,000

Children count by ones from a number, over the hundred, and into the next hundred. For example, 498, 499, 500, 501, 502, 503.

Mistakes often occur when counting this way, so watch for errors that children may make.

Some children will write 5003 instead of 503 for five hundred three. Using Secret Code Cards will help children write the numbers correctly.

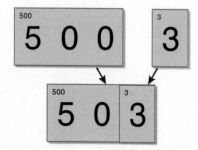

Counting aloud to 1,000 and grouping and labeling small objects provide written and oral practice, and are good ways to help children recognize the difference between 5,003 and 503.

Please call if you have any questions or concerns. Thank you for helping your child learn how to add 3-digit numbers by counting to 1,000.

Sincerely,
Your child's teacher

Estimada familia:

En esta unidad los niños están aprendiendo diferentes maneras de sumar números de 3 dígitos con totales de menos de 1,000, reagrupando y sin reagrupar. Una manera en que los niños sumarán números de 3 dígitos es contando hasta 1,000 de diez en diez y de cien en cien.

Contar hasta 1,000

Los niños cuentan de uno en uno a partir de un número, llegan a la centena y comienzan con la siguiente centena.

Por ejemplo, 498, 499, 500, 501, 502, 503.

Cuando se cuenta de esta manera los niños suelen cometer errores. Por lo tanto, preste atención a errores que los niños puedan cometer.

Algunos niños podrian escribir 5003 en vez de 503 al intentar escribir quinientos tres. Usar las Tarjetas de código secreto ayudará a los niños a escribir correctamente los números.

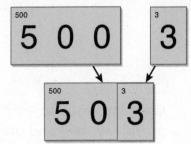

Contar hasta 1,000 en voz alta y poner objectos pequeños en grupos y rotularlos proporcionan práctica oral y escrita, y ayudan a los niños a reconocer la diferencia entre 5,003 y 503.

Si tiene alguna duda o pregunta, por favor comuníquese conmigo. Gracias por ayudar a su niño a aprender a sumar números de 3 dígitos contando hasta 1,000.

Atentamente,
El maestro de su niño

Class Activity

Name _____

▶ **Expanded Numbers**

Write the **hundreds**, **tens**, and **ones**.

1. 382 = <u>300</u> + <u>80</u> + <u>2</u>
   H T O

2. 738 = ____ + ____ + ____

3. 526 = ____ + ____ + ____

4. 267 = ____ + ____ + ____

Write the number.

5. 400 + 50 + 9 = <u>459</u>
                    H T O

6. 800 + 10 + 3 = _____

7. 100 + 70 + 5 = _____

8. 600 + 40 + 1 = _____

Write the missing number.
Watch the hundreds, tens, and ones.
They are out of order.

9. _____ = 5 + 900 + 40

10. 30 + 7 + 200 = _____

11. _____ = 400 + 6 + 80

12. 9 + 800 + 40 = _____

13. _____ = 70 + 4 + 300

14. 60 + 500 + 3 = _____

15. _____ = 2 + 400 + 90

16. 9 + 90 + 200 = _____

17. 462 = 2 + 400 + _____

18. _____ + 90 + 700 = 798

19. 523 = 20 + 3 + _____

20. _____ + 4 + 200 = 224

⟩ 21. **On the Back** Write or draw your own definition
     of hundreds, tens, and ones.

Name

Place Value

Class Activity

▶ **Count Over a Hundred by Ones and by Tens**

Count by ones. Write the numbers.

1. 396 397 <u>398</u> <u>399</u> <u>400</u> <u>401</u> 402 403 404 405 406

2. 594 595 ___ ___ ___ ___ ___ ___ ___ ___ 604

3. 297 298 ___ ___ ___ ___ ___ ___ ___ ___ 307

4. 495 ___ ___ ___ ___ ___ ___ ___ ___ ___ 505

5. 598 ___ ___ ___ ___ ___ ___ ___ ___ ___ 608

6. 697 ___ ___ ___ ___ ___ ___ ___ ___ ___ 707

Count by tens. Write the numbers.

7. 830 840 <u>850</u> <u>860</u> 870 880 890 900 910 920 930

8. 370 380 ___ ___ ___ ___ ___ ___ ___ ___ 470

9. 640 ___ ___ ___ ___ ___ ___ ___ ___ ___ 740

10. 580 ___ ___ ___ ___ ___ ___ ___ ___ ___ 680

11. 750 ___ ___ ___ ___ ___ ___ ___ ___ ___ 850

12. 460 ___ ___ ___ ___ ___ ___ ___ ___ ___ 560

▶ Read and Write Word Names for Numbers

You can read or write numbers with words or symbols.

1 one	11 eleven	10 ten	100 one hundred
2 two	12 twelve	20 twenty	200 two hundred
3 three	13 thirteen	30 thirty	300 three hundred
4 four	14 fourteen	40 forty	400 four hundred
5 five	15 fifteen	50 fifty	500 five hundred
6 six	16 sixteen	60 sixty	600 six hundred
7 seven	17 seventeen	70 seventy	700 seven hundred
8 eight	18 eighteen	80 eighty	800 eight hundred
9 nine	19 nineteen	90 ninety	900 nine hundred
			1,000 one thousand

Write each number.

1. one hundred twenty-five _____

2. four hundred fifty-eight _____

3. six hundred thirty-one _____

4. nine hundred sixty-two _____

5. eight hundred forty _____

6. seven hundred three _____

Write each word name.

7. 500 _____

8. 592 _____

9. 650 _____

10. 605 _____

11. 1,000 _____

Count by Ones and by Tens

Class Activity

Vocabulary

estimate
actual amount

▶ **Estimate the Number of Objects in a Container**

1. **Estimate** the number of objects.
   Then count the **actual amount**.

Estimate			Actual (Real Amount)		
Groups of 100	Groups of 10	Extra Ones	Groups of 100	Groups of 10	Extra Ones

2. Draw boxes, sticks, and circles to show the number of objects the class has.

Groups of 100 (boxes)	Groups of 10 (sticks)	Extra Ones (circles)

3. **On the Back** Use the picture. Estimate to find the answer. Then explain how you found your estimate.

Lynn and Ramón picked some apples. About how many apples did they pick?

Group into Hundreds

▶ **Add Numbers with 1, 2, and 3 Digits**

Solve.

1. 100 + 100 = _____   100 + 10 = _____   100 + 1 = _____

   200 + 200 = _____   200 + 20 = _____   200 + 2 = _____

   300 + 300 = _____   300 + 30 = _____   300 + 3 = _____

   400 + 400 = _____   400 + 40 = _____   400 + 4 = _____

   500 + 500 = _____   500 + 50 = _____   500 + 5 = _____

2. 600 + 200 = _____   20 + 600 = _____   2 + 600 = _____

   700 + 300 = _____   30 + 700 = _____   3 + 700 = _____

   800 + 100 = _____   10 + 800 = _____   1 + 800 = _____

   900 + 100 = _____   10 + 900 = _____   1 + 900 = _____

   100 + 900 = _____   90 + 100 = _____   9 + 100 = _____

3. 100 + 134 = _____   100 + 34 = _____   4 + 100 = _____

   200 + 245 = _____   200 + 45 = _____   200 + 5 = _____

   300 + 356 = _____   56 + 300 = _____   6 + 300 = _____

   400 + 467 = _____   400 + 67 = _____   400 + 7 = _____

   500 + 478 = _____   78 + 500 = _____   8 + 500 = _____

Add Ones, Tens, and Hundreds **349**

Class Activity

▶ **Solve and Discuss**

Solve each story problem. Use your Secret Code Cards
or Proof Drawings if you wish.

4. A camping club bought some raisins. They bought 3 cartons that had 100 bags each. They had 24 bags left from their last trip. How many bags of raisins does the club have?

☐ _____
label

5. Two friends want to make necklaces. They buy 1 package of a hundred red beads, 1 package of a hundred blue beads, and 1 package of a hundred green beads. They already have 12 loose beads. How many beads do they have altogether?

☐ _____
label

6. Mia and Bo want to advertise their yard sale. They decide to make flyers. They buy 2 packs of paper. Each pack has 200 sheets in it. They have 32 sheets in their art box. How many sheets of paper do they have?

☐ _____
label

7. All of the students at a school went out on the playground. They formed 8 groups of one hundred students and 6 groups of ten. There were 5 students left. How many students go to this school?

☐ _____
label

Add Ones, Tens, and Hundreds

Name _____

Class Activity

▶ **More Story Problems**

Solve each story problem.

8. The scout troop collected aluminum cans to recycle. They counted 2 groups of one hundred cans and 5 groups of ten. They had 7 more cans. How many cans did the troop collect?

[ ] _____
label

9. Angelica bought some toothpicks. She bought 8 packets of one hundred and 4 packets of ten. She already had 3 toothpicks. How many toothpicks does Angelica have in all?

[ ] _____
label

10. Dawn put up strings of lights in the yard. She used 4 strings that had one hundred lights on them. She also used 8 strings that had ten lights on them. How many lights did she use?

[ ] _____
label

11. Neil works at a newspaper stand. He counted 5 groups of one hundred newspapers and 3 groups of ten. He also counted 6 more loose newspapers. How many newspapers were at the stand?

[ ] _____
label

12. **On the Back** Write ten 3-digit numbers. Round each one to the nearest hundred. Tell whether you round up or down.

Add Ones, Tens, and Hundreds

Class Activity

Name _____

▶ **Review Coins**

Here are some coins and the amount of money they are worth.

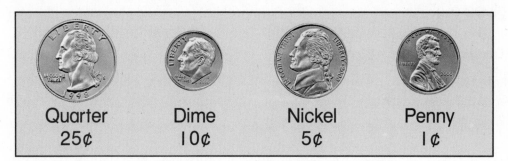

| Quarter | Dime | Nickel | Penny |
| 25¢ | 10¢ | 5¢ | 1¢ |

The Quarter Machine turns **quarters** into other coins. What coins might the machine give you that equal 25¢? Draw some different ways. Use a circle with the number of cents inside for each coin.

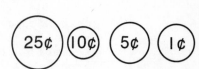

1.

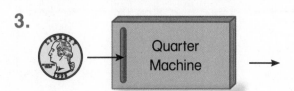

2.

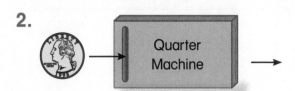

3.

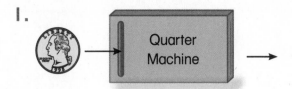

4.

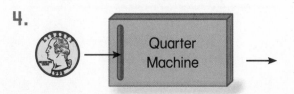

Going Further

Name _____

► **Coin Combinations**

For each Quarter Machine, draw a picture to
show the coins it gives out.

1.
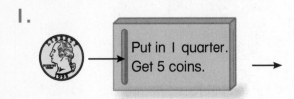
Put in 1 quarter.
Get 5 coins.

2.
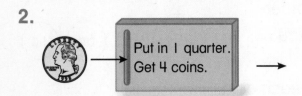
Put in 1 quarter.
Get 4 coins.

3.

Put in 1 quarter.
Get 7 coins.

4.

Put in 1 quarter.
Get 8 coins.

5.
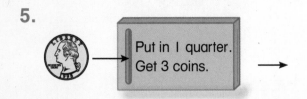
Put in 1 quarter.
Get 3 coins.

6.
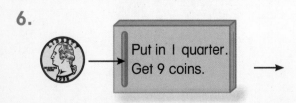
Put in 1 quarter.
Get 9 coins.

Review Quarters

Class Activity

Name _____

▶ **Buy and Sell Items**

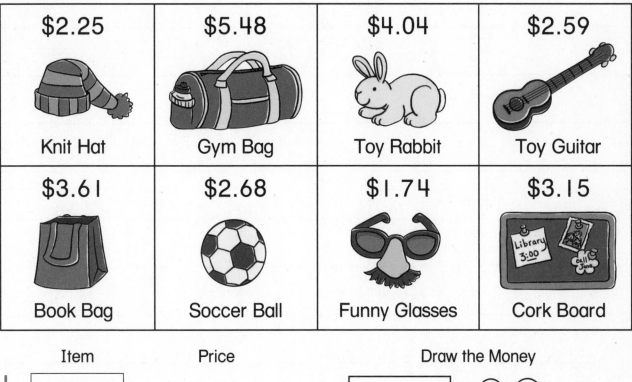

$2.25	$5.48	$4.04	$2.59
Knit Hat	Gym Bag	Toy Rabbit	Toy Guitar
$3.61	$2.68	$1.74	$3.15
Book Bag	Soccer Ball	Funny Glasses	Cork Board

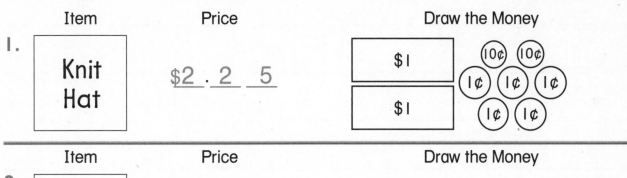

Item	Price	Draw the Money
1. Knit Hat	$2 . 2 5	$1 / $1 / 10¢ 10¢ / 1¢ 1¢ 1¢ / 1¢ 1¢

Item	Price	Draw the Money
2.	$ ___ . ___ ___	

Item	Price	Draw the Money
3.	$ ___ . ___ ___	

4. On the Back Make a list of the different ways you can make 80¢ using dimes and nickels.

Name _____

Buy with Dollars and Cents

Name _____

▶ **The Grocery Store**

8 Bananas $1.29	12 Muffins $.99	1 Can of Tuna $2.38	1 Bushel of Apples $4.37
1 Dozen Eggs $1.68	6 Slices of Pizza $3.49	1 Sandwich $1.54	1 Box of Tacos $2.46
4 Yogurts $2.25	1 Jar of Pickles $.57	3 Bunches of Grapes $1.79	6 Oranges $2.07
3 Boxes of Pasta $3.72	2 Cans of Soup $1.45	1 Pound of Nuts $3.48	1 Dozen Peaches $1.10

⮕ **On the Back** Write about a time you spent money on something. How much did you start with? How much money did you spend? How much money did you have left?

Change from $5.00

Class Activity

Name _____

▶ **Addition Sprint**

5 + 7 =	9 + 6 =	7 + 6 =
4 + 8 =	7 + 8 =	4 + 6 =
3 + 9 =	9 + 7 =	0 + 7 =
7 + 5 =	9 + 2 =	4 + 9 =
4 + 5 =	5 + 2 =	6 + 8 =
8 + 4 =	6 + 4 =	8 + 5 =
8 + 6 =	8 + 7 =	6 + 1 =
6 + 9 =	5 + 5 =	5 + 4 =
9 + 9 =	1 + 9 =	7 + 4 =
6 + 3 =	7 + 9 =	3 + 6 =
9 + 0 =	4 + 7 =	9 + 4 =
7 + 7 =	8 + 8 =	5 + 8 =
9 + 1 =	6 + 6 =	3 + 4 =
8 + 9 =	3 + 5 =	6 + 7 =
2 + 5 =	9 + 3 =	1 + 6 =
3 + 9 =	2 + 9 =	5 + 6 =
2 + 7 =	2 + 6 =	5 + 5 =
9 + 4 =	5 + 9 =	6 + 8 =
2 + 8 =	8 + 2 =	4 + 4 =.
0 + 8 =	9 + 8 =	1 + 8 =
8 + 3 =	6 + 5 =	6 + 7 =

► **Solve and Explain**

Solve each story problem.
Be ready to explain what you did.

1. Milo made a display of plant and fish fossils for the library. He put in 478 plant fossils. He put in 67 fish fossils. How many fossils were in the display?

   ☐ _____
        label

2. The nature club planted some pine and birch trees. They planted 496 birch trees. Then they planted 283 pine trees. How many trees did the club plant in all?

   ☐ _____
        label

3. There were 504 yellow ducks entered in the Rubber Duck River Race. Then we added 38 white ones. How many ducks are in the race now?

   ☐ _____
        label

4. There are 189 children at Camp Sunshine. There are 375 children at Camp Bluebird. How many children are there at the two camps?

   ☐ _____
        label

Name _____

Extra Practice

▶ **Solve and Discuss**

Add using any method. Make a proof drawing if it helps.

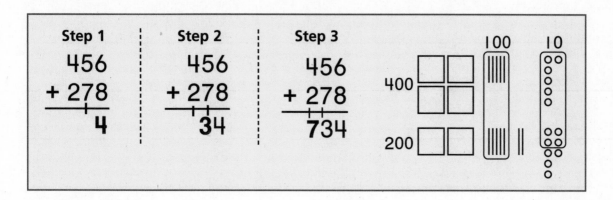

Step 1	Step 2	Step 3
456 + 278 ————— 4	456 + 278 ————— 34	456 + 278 ————— 734

1. 375
  + 482

2. 148
  + 236

3. 584
  + 361

4. 168
  + 674

5. 289
  + 376

6. 563
  + 157

7. 497
  + 259

8. 124
  + 563

9. 348
  + 239

10. **On the Back** Write two of your own story problems
for a classmate to solve.

Solve and Discuss

Dear Family,

Your child is now learning how to add 3-digit numbers. First, children do this with methods they invent themselves or they extend the drawings they did for 2-digit addition.

Children solve the great "mystery" of addition: a hundred can be made from the extra tens, and a ten can be made from the extra ones. *Math Expressions* shows children these two simple methods for 3-digit addition.

New Groups Below

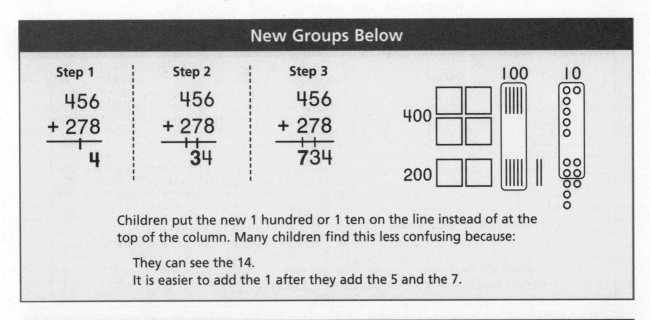

Children put the new 1 hundred or 1 ten on the line instead of at the top of the column. Many children find this less confusing because:

They can see the 14.
It is easier to add the 1 after they add the 5 and the 7.

Show All Totals

$$
\begin{array}{r}
456 \\
+\ 278 \\
\hline
\end{array}
$$

hundreds → 600
tens → 120
ones → 14

734

Children see the hundreds, tens, and ones they are adding. Children may also use the New Groups Above.

$$
\begin{array}{r}
\overset{1\ \ 1}{4}56 \\
+\ 278 \\
\hline
734
\end{array}
$$

These also can be seen when they make a math drawing like the one above.

Children may use any method that they understand, can explain, and can do fairly quickly. They should use hundreds, tens, and ones language to explain. This shows that they understand that they are adding 4 hundreds and 2 hundreds and not 4 and 2.

Please call if you have questions or comments.

Sincerely,
Your child's teacher

Estimada familia:

Ahora su niño está aprendiendo a sumar números de 3 dígitos. Primero, los niños hacen esto con métodos que ellos mismos inventan, o amplílan los dibujos que hicieron para la suma de números de dos dígitos.

Los niños resuelven el "misterio" de la suma: se puede formar una centena a partir de las decenas que sobran y se puede formar una decena a partir de las unidades que sobran. *Math Expressions* les muestra a los niños estos dos métodos simples de suma de números de tres dígitos.

Grupos nuevos abajo

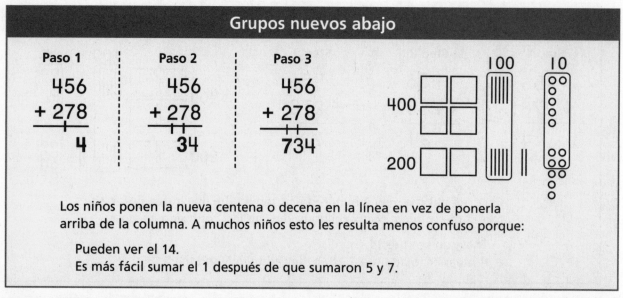

Paso 1	Paso 2	Paso 3
456	456	456
+ 278	+ 278	+ 278
4	34	734

Los niños ponen la nueva centena o decena en la línea en vez de ponerla arriba de la columna. A muchos niños esto les resulta menos confuso porque:

Pueden ver el 14.
Es más fácil sumar el 1 después de que sumaron 5 y 7.

Mostrar todos los totales

```
          456
        + 278
centenas → 600
decenas → 120
unidades → 14
          734
```

Los niños ven las centenas, las decenas y las unidades que están sumando. Los niños también pueden usar los Grupos nuevos arriba.

```
  456
+ 278
  734
```

Esto también se puede observar cuando hacen un dibujo matemático como el de arriba.

Los niños pueden usar cualquier método que comprendan, puedan explicar y puedan hacer relativamente rápido. Para explicar deben usar un lenguaje relacionado con centenas, decenas y unidades. Esto demuestra que entienden que están sumando 4 centenas y 2 centenas, y no 4 y 2.

Si tiene alguna duda o pregunta, por favor comuníquese conmigo.

Atentamente,
El maestro de su niño

Solve and Discuss

Class Activity

Name _____

► **Make a Table**

$1.86	$2.93	$4.67
Swan	Zebra	Leopard
$4.96	$2.68	$3.79
Bear	Raccoon	Elephant
$3.79	$1.55	$1.58
Kangaroo	Owl	Turtle
$4.94	$2.81	$3.57
Monkey	Penguin	Giraffe

Add Money Amounts **365**

▶ **Add 3-Digit Money Amounts**

1. Animals: _____

_____

$.

+ $. _____

Make a new ten?   _____

Make a new hundred? _____

2. Animals: _____

_____

$.

+ $. _____

Make a new ten?   _____

Make a new hundred? _____

3. Animals: _____

_____

$.

+ $. _____

Make a new ten?   _____

Make a new hundred? _____

4. Animals: _____

_____

$.

+ $. _____

Make a new ten?   _____

Make a new hundred? _____

5. Animals: _____

_____

$.

+ $. _____

Make a new ten?   _____

Make a new hundred? _____

6. Animals: _____

_____

$.

+ $. _____

Make a new ten?   _____

Make a new hundred? _____

Class Activity

► **Solve and Explain**

Add. Use any method. Make a Proof Drawing if you wish.

1.   2 3 6
    + 4 7 8

Make a new ten? _____

Make a new hundred? _____

2. 183 + 517 = _____

Make a new ten? _____

Make a new hundred? _____

3. 93 + 485 = _____

Make a new ten? _____

Make a new hundred? _____

4.   3 6 8
    + 2 5 7

Make a new ten? _____

Make a new hundred? _____

5. 347 + 37 = _____

Make a new ten? _____

Make a new hundred? _____

6. 645 + 87 = _____

Make a new ten? _____

Make a new hundred? _____

7. **On the Back** Write and solve a story problem using 3-digit numbers. Explain how you made a new ten or hundred to add the numbers.

Discuss 3-Digit Addition

Class Activity

► **Find the Hidden Animal**

Directions for the puzzle appearing on page 370.

1. Start by coloring in the six dotted squares. These are "free" squares. They are part of the puzzle solution.

2. Solve a problem below. Then look for the answer in the puzzle grid. Color it in.

3. Solve all 20 questions correctly. Color in all 20 correct answers.

4. Name the hidden picture. It is a(n) _____.

524 +247	287 +164	384 +375	456 +174	327 +265
207 +595	248 +376	282 +457	548 +387	233 +288
367 +265	293 +595	284 +376	295 +463	138 +327
286 + 78	407 +266	503 +148	78 +65	192 +339

Name _____

See page 369 for directions on how to solve the puzzle.

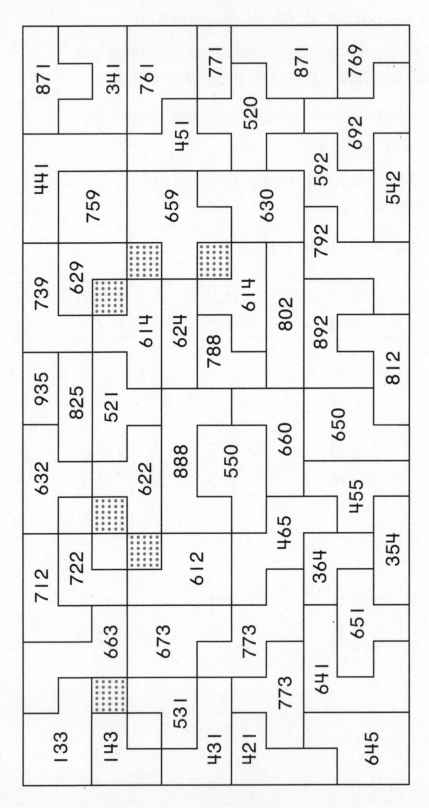

Discuss 3-Digit Addition

Class Activity

Name

▶ **Adding Up to Solve Story Problems**

Solve each story problem.   **Show your work.**

1. Mr. Cruz planted 750 yams to sell.
   After he sold some, he had 278 yams
   left. How many yams did he sell?

   ☐ _____
            label

2. Last year there were 692 houses in
   our town. This year some new
   houses were built. Now there are
   976 houses. How many new houses
   were built this year?

   ☐ _____
            label

3. Delia had 524 rocks in her collection.
   She gave some to her sister. Then
   she had 462 rocks. How many rocks
   did she give away?

   ☐ _____
            label

4. On Saturday, 703 people went to a
   movie. 194 went in the afternoon.
   The rest went in the evening. How
   many people went in the evening?

   ☐ _____
            label

5. **On the Back** Write a story problem with the answer **235 seashells.**

Story Problems: Unknown Addends

Name _____

▶ Subtraction Sprint

7 – 4 =	10 – 6 =	17 – 9 =
13 – 5 =	15 – 9 =	6 – 4 =
9 – 3 =	11 – 3 =	10 – 7 =
11 – 2 =	18 – 9 =	13 – 9 =
8 – 6 =	8 – 4 =	12 – 5 =
12 – 9 =	9 – 7 =	16 – 8 =
6 – 3 =	13 – 6 =	14 – 7 =
15 – 7 =	12 – 3 =	10 – 6 =
10 – 8 =	16 – 7 =	8 – 5 =
8 – 3 =	7 – 5 =	11 – 9 =
14 – 5 =	12 – 4 =	13 – 7 =
11 – 7 =	17 – 8 =	14 – 8 =
10 – 4 =	9 – 4 =	10 – 5 =
12 – 8 =	14 – 8 =	12 – 6 =
16 – 9 =	11 – 4 =	15 – 7 =
14 – 6 =	9 – 6 =	13 – 6 =
9 – 5 =	12 – 7 =	11 – 8 =
13 – 9 =	14 – 9 =	12 – 3 =
10 – 3 =	13 – 4 =	13 – 5 =
15 – 8 =	7 – 3 =	15 – 6 =
11 – 5 =	11 – 6 =	13 – 8 =

Name _____

▶ **Discuss Subtraction Problems**

Solve each story problem. Use any method.
Make a proof drawing.

1. A teacher bought 200 erasers for his students. He gave 152 of them away. How many erasers does he have left over?

2. The school cafeteria has 500 apples. Some of them were served with lunch. There are now 239 apples left. How many apples did the cafeteria serve?

☐ _____	☐ _____
label	label

3. Teresa sells pianos. She must sell 600 of them. She has already sold 359. How many does she have left to sell?

4. Jorge is on a basketball team. He scored 181 points last year. He scored some points this year too. He now has a total of 400 points. How many points did he score this year?

☐ _____	☐ _____
label	label

Story Problems with Hundreds Numbers

Dear Family,

Your child is now learning how to subtract 3-digit numbers. The most important part is understanding and being able to explain a method. Children may use any method that they understand, can explain, and can perform fairly quickly.

Expanded Method	Ungroup First Method

Expanded Method

	Step 1	Step 2
		300 + 120 + 12
432 =	400 + 30 + 2	4̶0̶0̶ + 3̶0̶ + 2̶
−273 =	−200 + 70 + 3	− 200 + 70 + 3

Step 3 { 100 + 50 + 9 = 159 }

Step 1 "Expand" each number to show that it is made up of hundreds, tens, and ones.

Step 2 Check to see if there are enough ones to subtract from. If not, ungroup a ten into 10 ones and add it to the existing ones. Check to see if there are enough tens to subtract from. If not, ungroup a hundred into 10 tens and add it to the existing tens. Children may also ungroup from the left.

Step 3 Subtract to find the answer. Children may subtract from left to right or right to left.

Ungroup First Method

$$3\overset{12}{\cancel{2}}12$$
$$432$$
$$-273$$

Ungroup from the right.

$$3\overset{12}{\cancel{2}}12$$
$$432$$
$$-273$$
$$\overline{159}$$

Subtract.

Step 1 Check to see if there are enough ones and tens to subtract from. Ungroup where needed.

Look inside 432. Ungroup 432 and rename it as 3 hundreds, 12 tens, and 12 ones.

Ungroup from the left:

$$3\overset{12}{\cancel{13}}12$$
$$432$$
$$-273$$
$$\overline{159}$$

Step 2 Subtract to find the answer. Children may subtract from the left or from the right.

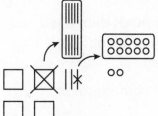

Ungroup

In explaining any method they use, children are expected to use "hundreds, tens, and ones" language to show that they understand place value.

Please call if you have questions or comments.

Sincerely,
Your child's teacher

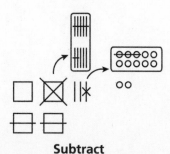

Subtract

Estimada familia:

Su niño está aprendiendo a restar números de 3 dígitos. Lo más importante es comprender y saber explicar un método. Los niños pueden usar cualquier método que comprendan, puedan explicar y puedan hacer relativamente rápido.

Método extendido

Paso 1 **Paso 2**

$$432 = 400 + 30 + 2$$
$$-273 = -200 + 70 + 3$$

Paso 3
$$100 + 50 + 9$$
$$= 159$$

Paso 1 "Extender" cada número para mostrar que consta de centenas, decenas y unidades.

Paso 2 Observar si hay suficientes unidades para restar. Si no, desagrupar una decena para formar 10 unidades y sumarlas a las unidades existentes. Observar si hay suficientes decenas para restar. Si no, desagrupar una centena para formar 10 decenas y sumarlas a las decenas existentes. Los niños también pueden desagrupar por la izquierda.

Paso 3 Restar para hallar la respuesta. Los niños pueden restar de izquierda a derecha o de derecha a izquierda.

Método de desagrupar primero

Desagrupar por la derecha   **Restar**

Paso 1 Observar si hay suficientes unidades y decenas para restar. Desagrupar cuando haga falta.

Mirar dentro de 432. Desagrupar 432 y volver a nombrarlo como 3 centenas, 12 decenas y 12 unidades.

Desagrupar por la izquierda:

Paso 2 Restar para hallar la respuesta. Los niños pueden restar empezando por la izquierda o por la derecha.

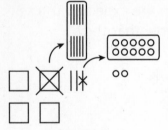

Desagrupar

Para explicar cualquier método que usen, los niños deben usar un lenguaje relacionado con centenas, decenas y unidades para demostrar que comprenden el valor posicional.

Si tiene alguna duda o comentario, por favor comuníquese conmigo.

Atentamente,
El maestro de su niño

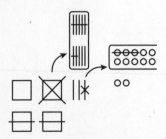

Restar

Story Problems with Hundreds Numbers

Class Activity

► **Represent a Subtraction Exercise**

Decide if you need to **ungroup** . If you need to ungroup, draw a magnifying glass around the top number. Then find the answer.

1.
```
  5 0 8
- 3 4 6
```

Ungroup to get 10 ones? _____

Ungroup to get 10 tens? _____

2.
```
  5 0 0
- 3 0 6
```

Ungroup to get 10 ones? _____

Ungroup to get 10 tens? _____

3.
```
  6 7 0
- 3 4 0
```

Ungroup to get 10 ones? _____

Ungroup to get 10 tens? _____

4.
```
  5 7 0
- 3 9 0
```

Ungroup to get 10 ones? _____

Ungroup to get 10 tens? _____

5. **On the Back** Write and solve your own story problem. Use the number **505** in your problem.

Subtract from Numbers with Zeros

► **Review Addition and Subtraction**

Ring *add* or *subtract.* Check if you need to ungroup or
make a new ten or hundred. Then find the answer.

1.
```
  7 6 2
- 3 9 5
```

Subtract

☐ Ungroup to get 10 ones

☐ Ungroup to get 10 tens

Add

☐ Make 1 new ten

☐ Make 1 new hundred

2.
```
  3 9 5
+ 3 6 7
```

Subtract

☐ Ungroup to get 10 ones

☐ Ungroup to get 10 tens

Add

☐ Make 1 new ten

☐ Make 1 new hundred

3.
```
  2 8 7
- 1 9 3
```

Subtract

☐ Ungroup to get 10 ones

☐ Ungroup to get 10 tens

Add

☐ Make 1 new ten

☐ Make 1 new hundred

4.
```
  4 3 7
+ 3 2 4
```

Subtract

☐ Ungroup to get 10 ones

☐ Ungroup to get 10 tens

Add

☐ Make 1 new ten

☐ Make 1 new hundred

5. **On the Back** Explain how you know when to ungroup
in subtraction. Use the words *ones, tens,* and *hundreds.*

Relationships between Addition and Subtraction Methods

Class Activity

Name _____

► **Subtraction Sprint**

7 − 4 =	10 − 6 =	17 − 9 =
13 − 5 =	15 − 9 =	6 − 4 =
9 − 3 =	11 − 3 =	10 − 7 =
11 − 2 =	18 − 9 =	13 − 9 =
8 − 6 =	8 − 4 =	12 − 5 =
12 − 9 =	9 − 7 =	16 − 8 =
6 − 3 =	13 − 6 =	14 − 7 =
15 − 7 =	12 − 3 =	10 − 6 =
10 − 8 =	16 − 7 =	8 − 5 =
8 − 3 =	7 − 5 =	11 − 9 =
14 − 5 =	12 − 4 =	13 − 7 =
11 − 7 =	17 − 8 =	14 − 8 =
10 − 4 =	9 − 4 =	10 − 5 =
12 − 8 =	14 − 8 =	12 − 6 =
16 − 9 =	11 − 4 =	15 − 7 =
14 − 6 =	9 − 6 =	13 − 6 =
9 − 5 =	12 − 7 =	11 − 8 =
13 − 9 =	14 − 9 =	12 − 3 =
10 − 3 =	13 − 4 =	13 − 5 =
15 − 8 =	7 − 3 =	15 − 6 =
11 − 5 =	11 − 6 =	13 − 8 =

Class Activity

Vocabulary

unknown start problem
comparison problem

▶ **Solve Complex Story Problems**

Solve the **unknown start** and **comparison problems**.

1. Marian had a collection of miniature cars. Then she gave 465 cars to her brother Simon. Now Marian has 288 cars. How many cars did she have to begin with?

[____] _____
label

2. In September the Shaws planted some bulbs. In October they planted 178 more bulbs. Altogether they planted 510 bulbs. How many bulbs did they plant in September?

[____] _____
label

3. Lila has 288 mugs in her collection, which is 158 fewer than her friend Letty has. How many mugs does Letty have in her collection?

[____] _____
label

4. One year the Ricos planted 640 flowers. This was 243 more than the Smiths planted. How many flowers did the Smiths plant?

[____] _____
label

Class Activity

▶ **Solve and Discuss**

Solve each story problem.

1. Lucero spilled a bag of marbles. 219 fell on the floor. 316 were still in the bag. How many were in the bag before it spilled?

   [ ] _____ label

2. Al counted bugs in the park. He counted 561 on Monday. He counted 273 fewer than that on Tuesday. How many bugs did he count on both days combined?

   [ ] _____ label

3. Happy the Clown gives out balloons. She gave out 285 at the zoo and then she gave out some more at the amusement park. Altogether she gave out 503. How many balloons did she give out at the amusement park?

   [ ] _____ label

4. Charlie the Clown gave out 842 balloons at the fun fair. He gave out 194 at the store. He gave out 367 at the playground. How many more balloons did he give out at the fun fair than at the playground?

   [ ] _____ label

Extra Practice

Name _____

▶ **Practice Story Problems**

Solve. Show your work on a separate sheet of paper.

1. Damon collects stamps. He had 383 stamps. Then he bought 126 more at a yard sale. How many stamps does he have now?

   ☐ _____
   label

2. Mr. Lewis sold 438 melons yesterday. Now he has 294 melons left to sell. How many melons did he have to start?

   ☐ _____
   label

3. Ali is passing out ribbons for a race. She passed out 57 ribbons so far and she has 349 ribbons left. How many ribbons did she have at the start?

   ☐ _____
   label

4. Tanya is doing a puzzle. She has put together 643 pieces. There are 1,000 pieces in the puzzle. How many pieces are left to put together?

   ☐ _____
   label

5. Pawel passed out fliers to advertise a play. He passed out 194 fliers at the bakery. He passed out 358 at the grocery store. How many more fliers did he pass out at the grocery store than at the bakery?

   ☐ _____
   label

6. Cora collected 542 sports cards last year. She collected 247 fewer than that this year. How many cards did she collect in both years together?

   ☐ _____
   label

Mixed Addition and Subtraction Story Problems

Class Activity

Name _____

▶ The Yard Sale

Choose any two toys to buy. Pay for them with $10.00.

$4.87	$3.49	$2.59	$1.64
Baseball Glove	Globe	Perfume	Funny Glasses
$1.55	$2.48	$4.86	$3.97
Toy Binoculars	Toy Lamb	Ring	Toy Guitar

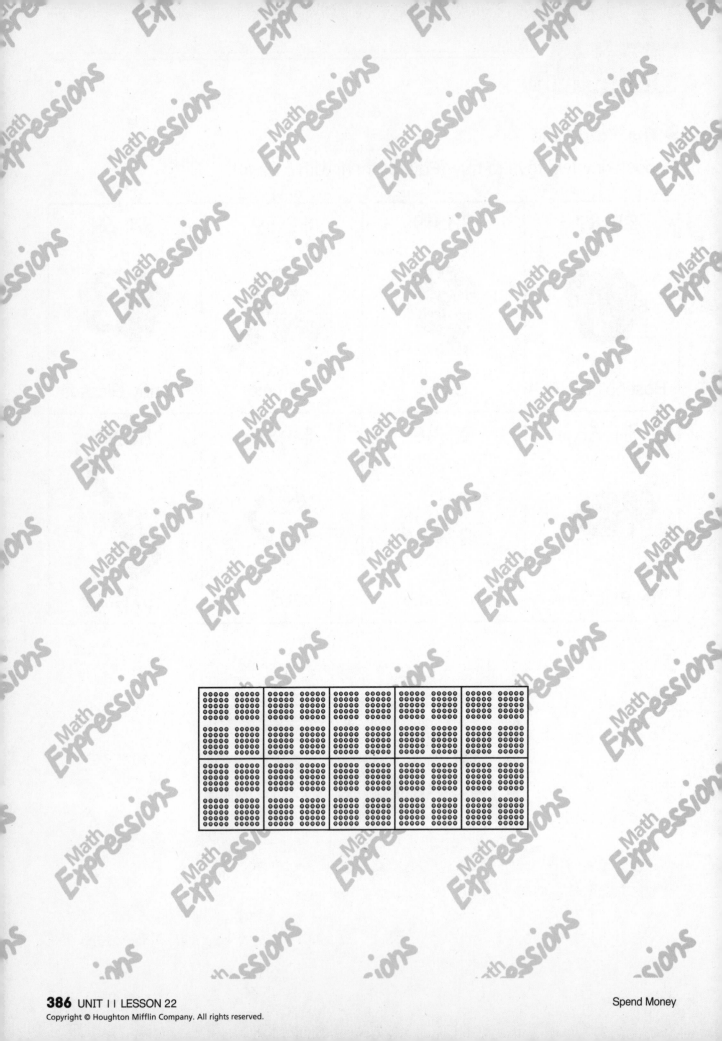

Spend Money

Going Further

▶ Introduce Front-End Estimation

Follow these steps to use front-end estimation.

- Keep the front digit of each number.
- Use zeros for all the other digits.
- Add or subtract according to the sign.

1.
$$53 \longrightarrow 50$$
$$+21 \longrightarrow +20$$

The estimate is _____ .

2.
$$53 \longrightarrow 50$$
$$-22 \longrightarrow -\underline{}$$

The estimate is _____ .

3.
$$686 \longrightarrow 600$$
$$+239 \longrightarrow +\underline{}$$

The estimate is _____ .

4.
$$686 \longrightarrow 600$$
$$-249 \longrightarrow -\underline{}$$

The estimate is _____ .

▶ Practice Using Front-End Estimation

Estimate each sum or difference. Use front-end estimation.

5.
$$64 \longrightarrow$$
$$+53 \longrightarrow +\underline{}$$

The estimate is _____ .

6.
$$842 \longrightarrow$$
$$-367 \longrightarrow -\underline{}$$

The estimate is _____ .

➡ **7. On the Back** Explain how you could use front-end estimation to choose the correct answer.

$$34 - 15 = \boxed{}$$ ○ 58 ○ 19 ○ 49 ○ 4

Spend Money

Name _____

▶Math and Art

In many cultures beads are woven in geometric patterns to make hatbands, belts, necklaces, and other items.
Find the shapes in these beadwork items.

You have learned to describe a pattern using letters.
The pattern below is an ABB pattern.

1. Make a hatband design with shapes.
   Use an ABAB pattern. Draw your design here.

2. Make a belt designs with shapes.
   Make an AAB pattern. Draw your design here.

3. Make a design with shapes for another item.
   Use any pattern you like.
   Describe your pattern with letters. _____

Name _____

▶**Following Directions**

1. Follow the directions. Use pattern blocks.

   A. Put the yellow hexagon on the line. Place one of its sides on the line.

   B. Put green triangles to the right and left of the hexagon. Place one side of each triangle on the line. Let another side of each triangle touch the side of the hexagon.

   C. Put an orange square on top of the hexagon. Place one side of the square on one side of the hexagon.

   _____

2. Trace the pattern blocks to show your work.

3. Use pattern blocks to make a design.

   A. Write directions for making your design on a separate sheet of paper.

   B. Give the directions to your partner to follow.

   C. Did your partner make your design? Explain.

   _____

   _____

Use Mathematical Processes

Name _____

1. Write the total.

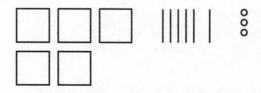

Total _____

2. Use boxes, sticks, and circles to show 478.

Total 478

Write the hundreds, tens, and ones.

Example: 456 = 400 + 50 + 6

3. 975 = _____ + _____ + _____

4. 283 = _____ + _____ + _____

---

5. Count by ones. Write the numbers.

294 295 ____ ____ ____ ____ ____ ____ ____ 304

6. Count by tens. Write the numbers.

330 340 ____ ____ ____ ____ ____ ____ ____ 430

<u>Name</u> _____

How much money is shown here? Use $ in your answer.

7.   _____

8.   _____

Add.

9.　7 4 5
　+1 3 8

10.　3 7 7
　+5 6 2

11.　4 8 8
　+3 5 4

12. 198 + 56 = _____

13. $3.98 + $2.81 = _____

14. $1.59 + $0.75 = _____

Subtract.

15.　6 1 8
　−4 7 3

16.　7 8 2
　−5 2 8

17.　4 4 7
　−1 7 8

Test

Subtract.

18. 5 0 5
    − 3 7 1
    _____

19. 3 0 0
    − 2 3 9
    _____

20. $ 1 0 . 0 0
    − $ 4 . 8 1
    _____

21. $10.00 − $2.72 = _____

Solve.   Show your work.

22. Dena picked 472 apples. She sold
    187 at the Farmers Market. How
    many apples did she have left?

    ┌──────────┐
    │   │ _____
    └──────────┘   label

23. This morning 256 books were
    returned to the library. 596 more
    were returned this afternoon.
    How many books were returned
    altogether?

    ┌──────────┐
    │   │ _____
    └──────────┘   label

Solve.   **Show your work.**

24. Ada read 124 pages in a book. The
    book has 300 pages. How many
    more pages does she still have to
    read to finish the book?

    +-----------+ _____
    | |
    +-----------+
                    label

25. **Extended Response** Write and solve an addition or
    subtraction story problem using the numbers
    458 and 279.

    _____

    _____

    _____

    _____

    _____

    _____

    _____

    _____

    _____

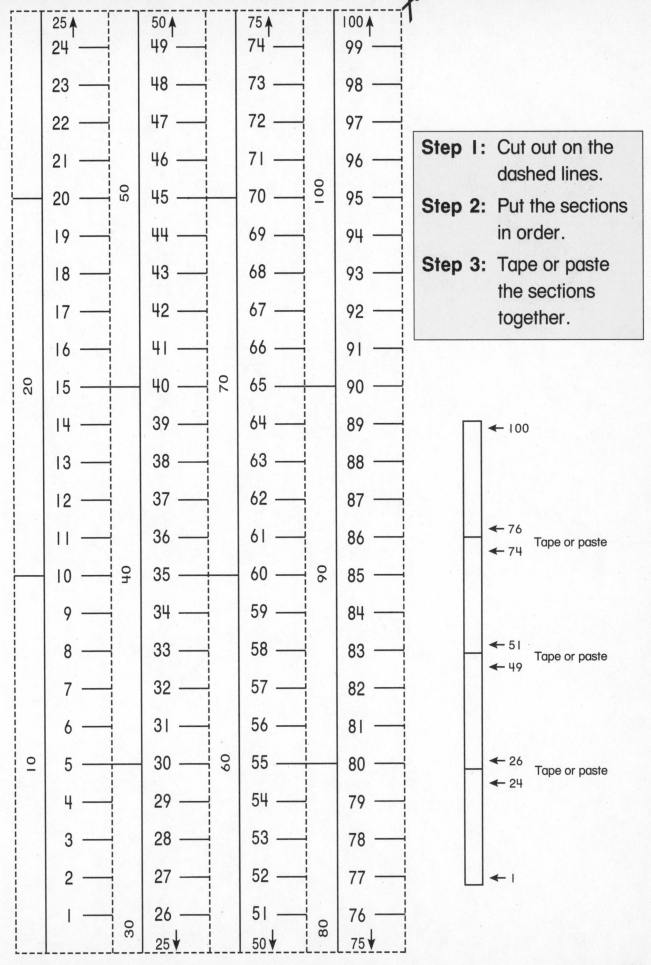

Step 1: Cut out on the dashed lines.

Step 2: Put the sections in order.

Step 3: Tape or paste the sections together.

← 100

← 76
Tape or paste
← 74

← 51
Tape or paste
← 49

← 26
Tape or paste
← 24

← 1

Meter Stick

▶ **Estimate and Measure**

Find a part of your hand that is about the length of each measure.

1. 1 cm _____

2. 1 dm _____

Find a part of your body that is about 1 meter long.

3. 1 m _____

Find the real object. Estimate and measure its length. Round if necessary.

4.

Estimate: about _____ cm

Measure: _____ cm

5.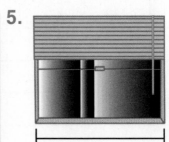

Estimate: about _____ cm

Measure: _____ cm

6.

Estimate: about _____ dm

Measure: _____ dm

7.

Estimate: about _____ m

Measure: _____ m

Draw a line segment to show each length.

8. 1 cm

9. 1 dm

Name _____

Class Activity

▶ Measure Heights

When you measure a length greater than 1 m, you
place two meter sticks end-to-end. The first meter stick
is 100 cm. You add 100 to the number of centimeters
you read from the second meter stick.

10. Complete the table for each person in your group.

Person's Name	Estimated Height (cm)	Actual Height (cm)	Difference Between Estimated and Actual Height (cm)

Use the data you collected to answer these questions.

11. Who is the tallest person in your group?

   _____

12. How much taller is the tallest person than the

   shortest person? _____

13. Whose estimated height was closest to his or her

   actual height? _____

14. On a separate sheet of paper, write four more questions
   you could ask about this data. Trade your questions with
   another group and answer each other's questions.

Meters and Decimeters

Dear Family,

In this geometry unit, your child will measure in centimeters, meters, and decimeters. Children develop a sense of the size of each metric unit by finding personal or body referents, drawing line segments, and measuring objects and distances with a meter stick.

Children compare the metric units for length to the U.S. monetary system, both of which use the base ten number system.

1 decimeter = 10 centimeters	1 dime = 10 cents
1 meter = 10 decimeters	1 dollar = 10 dimes
1 meter = 100 centimeters	1 dollar = 100 cents

Children convert units of linear measurement and units of the monetary system. They solve story problems to strengthen their understanding of the base ten system, while reinforcing their skills in the addition of 3-digit numbers.

The last two lessons of this unit introduce children to three-dimensional shapes. They use unit cubes to build rectangular prisms, and they draw these prisms from the top, side, and front view. They also learn how to find the volume of a three-dimensional shape by counting unit cubes.

In the last lesson, children look at attributes of three-dimensional shapes, like vertices, faces, and edges.

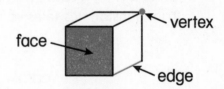

Children also investigate how different three-dimensional shapes stack and if they roll or slide across a surface. They then sort three-dimensional shapes by attributes.

If you have any questions or comments, please call or write to me.

Sincerely,
Your child's teacher

Estimada familia:

En esta unidad sobre geometría, su niño medirá con centímetros, metros y decímetros. Los niños van a comprender el tamaño de cada unidad métrica usando el cuerpo como punto de referencia, dibujando segmentos de recta y midiendo objetos y distancias con una regla de un metro.

Los niños van a comparar las unidades métricas de longitud con el sistema monetario de los EE. UU., ya que ambos utilizan el sistema de base diez.

1 decímetro = 10 centímetros	1 moneda de 10¢ = 10 centavos
1 metro = 10 decímetros	1 dólar = 10 monedas de 10¢
1 metro = 100 centímetros	1 dólar = 100 centavos

Los niños van a convertir unidades de longitud y unidades del sistema monetario. También resolverán problemas para reforzar su comprensión del sistema de base diez, a la vez que refuerzan su habilidad de sumar números de 3 dígitos.

Las dos últimas lecciones de esta unidad presentan las figuras tridimensionales. Los niños usarán cubos de unidad para construir prismas rectangulares y dibujarán los prismas desde arriba, desde el lado y desde adelante. También aprenderán cómo se calcula el volumen de una figura tridimensional contando cubos de unidad.

En la última lección, los niños estudiar los atributos de figuras tridimensionales tales como vértices, caras y aristas.

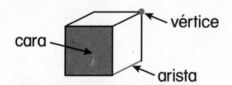

También verán cómo se pueden apilar las figuras tridimensionales y si ruedan o se deslizan sobre una superficie. Luego clasificarán las figuras tridimensionales según sus atributos.

Si tiene alguna duda o comentario, por favor comuníquese conmigo.

Atentamente,
El maestro de su niño

Class Activity

Vocabulary

centimeter (cm)
decimeter (dm)
meter (m)

▶ Equivalent Metric Lengths

1. Draw a line segment 10 **cm** long.

2. Draw a line segment 1 **dm** long.

3. What do you notice about the measurements 10 cm and 1 dm?

   _____

4. Fill in the correct number: 1 dm = _____ cm

5. Work in partners. One partner shows 1 m on a meter stick and the other partner shows 10 dm on a meter stick. What do you notice about the measurements 1 **m** and 10 dm?

   _____

6. Fill in the correct number: 1 m = _____ dm

7. Work in partners. Find 1 m and then 100 cm on a meter stick. What do you notice about the measurements 1 m and 100 cm?

   _____

Fill in the correct unit of measurement.

8. 1 _____ = 10 cm

9. 1 _____ = 10 dm

10. 1 _____ = 100 cm

Class Activity

▶ Jumping Game

In this game, you will stand at a start line and jump as far as possible.

Step 1: One person at a time, stand with toes at the start line.

Step 2: Jump as far as you can.

Step 3: Have another member in your group mark where your toes landed and measure the distance from the start line, in centimeters.

Step 4: Record the results in the table below.

Step 5: After everyone has jumped once, take a second turn.

Jumping Game		
Name	**First turn**	**Second turn**

11. Who jumped the farthest? _____

12. How many people jumped farther than 50 cm? _____

13. On a separate sheet of paper, write three more comparison questions about the data you collected. Share your questions with the group and answer them together.

Fun With Measuring

Name _____

Class Activity

▶ Guessing Game

In this game, you and a partner will write clues that describe rectangular objects in the classroom. You will trade clues with another pair and try to find their objects.

> **Step 1:** Measure the length and width of 3 objects. Record your measurements in the table below.

Object Dimensions		
Object	**Length (cm)**	**Width (cm)**

> **Step 2:** Write 2 clues that describe each object.
> Clue 1: Write the object's length and width.
> Clue 2: Describe the object by color, location, shape, or use.
> **Step 3:** Write the name of the object on the back of the index card.

What Am I?
Clue 1: I am 67 cm long and 44 cm wide.
Clue 2: I usually hang on the wall at the front of the classroom.

Answer

bulletin board

> **Step 4:** Read your clues to another pair. Ask them to guess each of your objects by first estimating and then measuring to check.

▶ Penny Toss Game

In this game, you will stand at the start line and toss
a penny as close as possible to the goal line.

Step 1: Take turns tossing a penny as close as possible to the goal line.
Step 2: Measure the distance of your toss in centimeters from the goal line.
Step 3: Complete the table below.

Penny Toss Game	
Name	**Distance from the goal line (cm)**

14. Whose penny landed closest to the goal line?

_____

15. How many children's pennies landed less than
    10 cm from the goal line? _____

16. On a separate sheet of paper, write three more
    comparison questions about the data you collected.
    Share your questions with the group and answer
    them together.

Fun With Measuring

Name _____

▶ **Money and Length Equivalencies**

Answer each question. Draw a picture if you need to.

1. How many ones in

   1 ten? _____

2. How many dimes in

   1 dollar? _____

3. How many pennies in

   1 dime? _____

4. How many tens in

   1 hundred? _____

5. How many centimeters in

   1 dm? _____

6. How many cents in

   1 dime? _____

7. How many pennies in

   1 dollar? _____

8. How many ones in

   1 hundred? _____

9. Write the numbers.

5 m   8 dm   4 cm

= _____ dm   4 cm

= _____ cm

_____ m _____ dm _____ cm

= 41 dm   2 cm

= _____ cm

$3.18

= _____ dimes _____ pennies

= _____ pennies

$ _____

= _____ dimes _____ pennies

= 412 pennies

10. **On the Back** Draw a picture to show the relationship between metric lengths (meters, decimeters, centimeters) and money (dollars, dimes, pennies).

Practice with Meters and Money

Name

▶ Rectangular Prisms

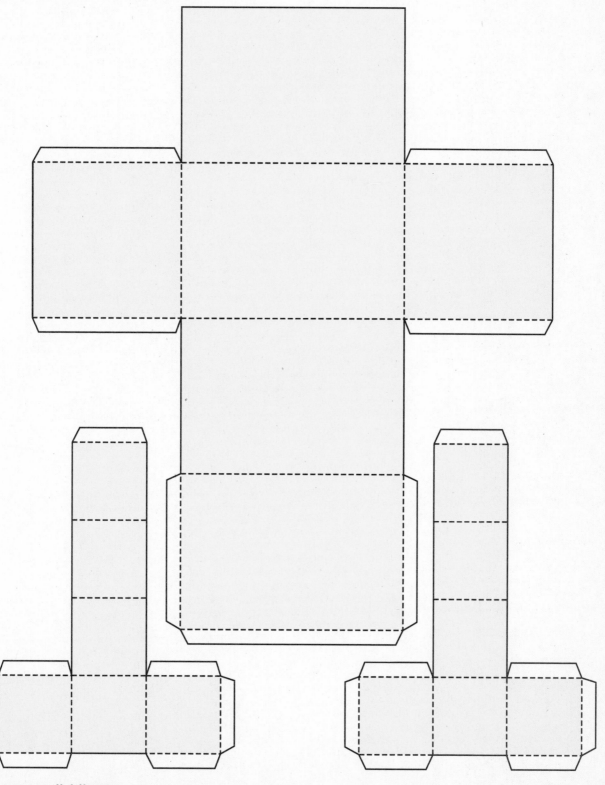

Cut on solid lines.
Fold on dashed lines.

Rectangular Prisms **407**

Class Activity

Name _____

Vocabulary
rectangular prism
views

▶ Build and Draw Rectangular Prisms

Using unit cubes, build a **rectangular prism** to match each description. Draw the rectangular prism from the top, front, and side **views**.

1. two rows of three unit cubes

      top view   **front view**   **side view**

2. one row of two unit cubes stacked on top of another row of two unit cubes

      top view   **front view**   **side view**

▶ Build Rectangular Prisms from Drawings

Build a rectangular prism to match each set of views.

3.

      top view   **front view**   **side view**

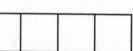

4.

      top view   **front view**   **side view**

Class Activity

Vocabulary

volume
cubic units

▶ Volume of 3-Dimensional Shapes

The **volume** of a 3-dimensional shape is the amount of space it occupies.

To measure volume, you can find the number of **cubic units** that make up the 3-dimensional shape.

1 cubic unit

Find the volume of each shape in cubic units.

5.

_____ cubic units

6.
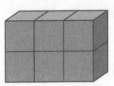
_____ cubic units

7.
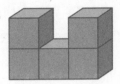
_____ cubic units

8.

_____ cubic units

9.
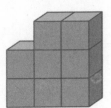
_____ cubic units

10.
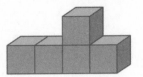
_____ cubic units

Use unit cubes to build each 3-dimensional shape. Find the volume by counting cubic units.

11.

_____ cubic units

12.

_____ cubic units

13.
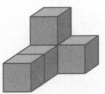
_____ cubic units

Name _____

Vocabulary

three-dimensional (3-D)

▶ **Identify Solid Shapes**

Name each **three-dimensional (3-D)** shape.

1.

_____

2.

_____

3.

_____

4.

_____

5.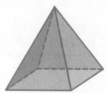

_____

6.

_____

7. Hunt for shapes in your classroom. Find examples of each shape and list them in the table below.

Shape	Examples
cone	
cube	
rectangular prism	
sphere	
square pyramid	
cylinder	

Analyze 3-Dimensional Shapes **411**

Class Activity

Name _____

Vocabulary
stack
slide
roll

► **Stack, Slide, and Roll**

You can **stack** some shapes.

You can **slide** some shapes.

You can **roll** some shapes.

8. Experiment with three-dimensional shapes to find out if you can stack, slide, or roll them. Place a checkmark in the column that applies to each shape.

Shape	Stack	Slide	Roll
cube			
square pyramid			
cone			
cylinder			
rectangular prism			
sphere			

Analyze 3-Dimensional Shapes

Class Activity

Name _____

▶ **Alike and Different**

Describe how each pair of shapes is alike and different.

Shapes	How these shapes are alike	How these shapes are different
9.		
10.		
11.		
12.		

Name _____

▶ **Sort Three-Dimensional Shapes**

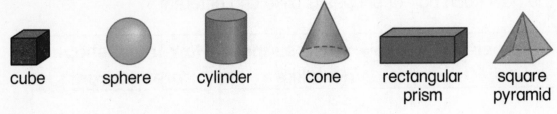

cube   sphere   cylinder   cone   rectangular prism   square pyramid

13. Choose your own sorting rule to sort these three-dimensional shapes into two groups.

My sorting rule is _____

The shapes _____

_____

The shapes _____

_____

▶ **Venn Diagram**

14. Sort the shapes above into two groups: shapes that have a rectangular face and shapes that have a circle face. Write the names of the shapes in the Venn diagram.

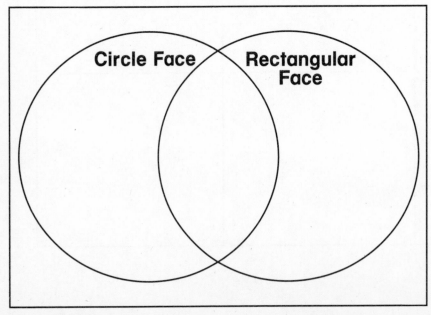

Circle Face   Rectangular Face

Write the numbers.

1. 170 cm = _____ m _____ dm

2. 654 cm = _____ m _____ dm _____ cm

3. 575 cm = _____ m _____ dm _____ cm

Is each shape **2-D (two-dimensional)** or
3-D (three-dimensional)?

4.   _____

5.   _____

6. Draw the top, front, and side views.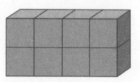

Top View   **Front View**   **Side View**

Find the volume of each shape in cubic units.

7.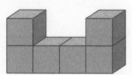

_____ cubic units

8.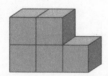

_____ cubic units

9. Sort the shapes. Write the names of the shapes in the Venn diagram.

cube   sphere   cylinder   cone   rectangular   square
                                                    prism   pyramid

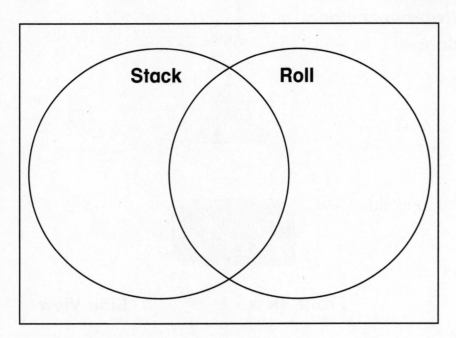

Stack   **Roll**

10. **Extended Response** Explain how knowing about ones, tens, and hundreds can help you write 138 centimeters as meters, decimeters, and centimeters.

_____

_____

_____

_____

Class Activity

Name _____

▶ **Practice Multiplication**

I have 5 vases. There are 2 flowers in each vase.

1 2   3 4   5 6   7 8   9 10

$5 \times 2 =$ __10__

2 + 2 + 2 + 2 + 2 = __10__

Write the addition and **multiplication** equation for each story. Make a math drawing to help you solve the problem.

---

1. I have 4 cats. Each cat has 3 toy mice. How many mice are there?

   $3 + 3 + 3 + 3 =$ _____

   $4 \times 3 =$ _____

   ☐ _____
   label

---

2. I eat 4 pieces of fruit every day. How many pieces of fruit do I eat in 5 days?

   ___ + ___ + ___ + ___ + ___ = _____

   $5 \times 4 =$ _____

   ☐ _____
   label

---

3. I have 3 packs of pencils. There are 5 pencils in each pack. How many pencils do I have?

   $5 + 5 + 5 =$ _____

   _____ × _____ = _____

   ☐ _____
   label

Class Activity

Vocabulary

count by
count-bys

▶ 2s Count-Bys

Ring each pair.

4. Fill in the chart below to make groups of 2. Ring each pair.
Then **count by** 2s by saying the last number in each group.

1	2
3	4
	10
	16

5. Write out the 2s **count-bys** below.

_____ 2 _____ 4 _____ _____ _____ 10 _____ _____ _____ 16 _____ _____

Introduction to Multiplication

Name _____

► **Count by 2s to Multiply**

Count by 2s. Then multiply.

6. Beach balls on a seal's nose

$4 \times 2 =$ ____8____

___ ___ ___ ___

7. Humps on a camel

$3 \times 2 =$ _____

___ ___ ___

8. Ice cubes in a pitcher

$6 \times 2 =$ _____

___ ___ ___ ___ ___ ___

9. Funny shoes on a clown

$5 \times 2 =$ _____

___ ___ ___ ___ ___

Going Further

▶ Draw Pictures and Write Equations

Draw a picture. Write the multiplication equation.

1. 1 bag of 2 marbles

$1 \times 2 =$ _____

2. 2 bags of 1 marble

$2 \times 1 =$ _____

3. 1 bag of 3 marbles

_____

4. 3 bags of 1 marble

_____

5. 1 bag of 5 marbles

_____

6. 5 bags of 1 marble

_____

7. What pattern do you see? Draw or write to explain.

Introduction to Multiplication

Dear Family,

In this unit, children are introduced to multiplication in three ways.

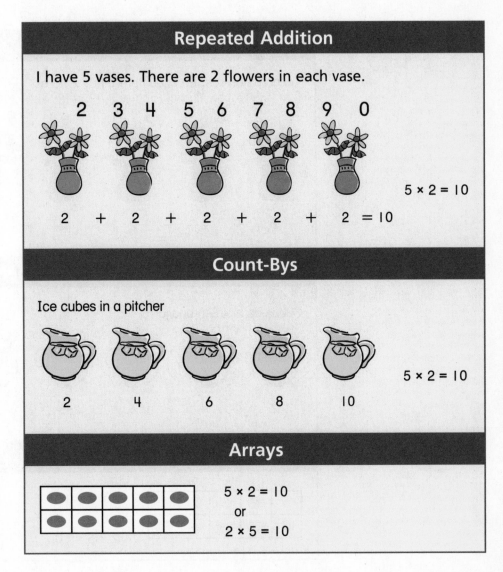

Please call if you have any questions or comments. Thank you for helping your child learn about multiplication.

Sincerely,
Your child's teacher

Estimada familia:

En esta unidad se la multiplicación de tres maneras.

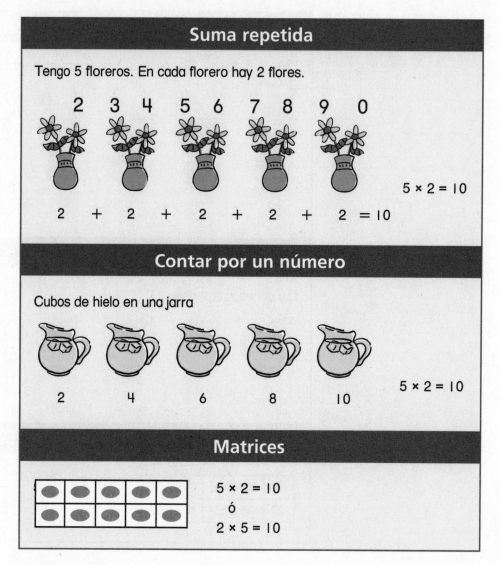

Suma repetida

Tengo 5 floreros. En cada florero hay 2 flores.

2 3 4 5 6 7 8 9 0

$5 \times 2 = 10$

2 + 2 + 2 + 2 + 2 = 10

Contar por un número

Cubos de hielo en una jarra

2   4   6   8   10

$5 \times 2 = 10$

Matrices

$5 \times 2 = 10$
ó
$2 \times 5 = 10$

Si tiene alguna duda o comentario, por favor comuníquese conmigo. Gracias por ayudar a su niño a aprender sobre la multiplicación.

Atentamente,
El maestro de su niño

Introduction to Multiplication

Class Activity

Vocabulary

count by
count-bys

▶ **3s Count-Bys**

1. Fill in the chart below to make groups of 3. Then
   count by 3s by saying the last number in each group.

1	2	3
4	5	6
		15
	20	
		27

2. Write out the 3s **count-bys** below.

___3___ ___6___ _____ _____ ___15___ _____ _____ _____ ___27___ _____

Class Activity

Name _____

▶ **Count by 3s to Multiply**

Count by 3s. Then **multiply**.

3. Sides on a triangle

$4 \times 3 = $ ___12___

——— ——— ——— ———

4. Fried eggs on a plate

$2 \times 3 = $ _____

——— ———

5. Leaves on a branch

$8 \times 3 = $ _____

6. Leaves on a shamrock

$9 \times 3 = $ _____

7. Holes in a bowling ball

$7 \times 3 = $ _____

——— ——— ——— ———

Groups of Three

▶ Hats for Sale

Use the pictograph to answer the questions.

Hats for Sale

Green	🎩 🎩 🎩
Red	🎩 🎩
Blue	🎩
Yellow	🎩 🎩

Key: Each 🎩 **= 3 hats**

1. How many hats does each 🎩 stand for?

☐ _____
label

2. How many red hats are for sale?

☐ _____
label

3. How many blue hats are for sale?

☐ _____
label

4. The store has 6 purple hats. How many symbols are needed to show the purple hats on the pictograph?

☐ _____
label

5. **On the Back** Write the answer and show your work for the following problem.

If each 🎩 stands for only 2 hats, how many symbols do you need to show the red hats?

Groups of Three **425**

Groups of Three

Class Activity

Name _____

Vocabulary
count by
count-bys

▶ 4s Count-Bys

1. Fill in the chart below to make groups of 4. Then **count by** 4s by saying the last number in each group.

1	2	3	4
5	6	7	8
	18		
			32

2. Write out the 4s **count-bys** below.

<u> 4 </u> <u> 8 </u> <u>   </u> <u> 20 </u> <u>   </u> <u>   </u> <u> 32 </u> <u>   </u> <u>   </u>

Class Activity

▶ **Count by 4s to Multiply**

Count by 4s. Then multiply.

3. Sides of a square

___ ___ ___ ___ ___

$5 \times 4 =$ _____

4. Legs on a lion

___ ___ ___ ___ ___ ___ ___

$7 \times 4 =$ _____

5. Strings on a violin

___ ___

$2 \times 4 =$ _____

6. Holes in a button

___ ___ ___ ___ ___ ___ ___ ___ ___

$9 \times 4 =$ _____

7. Cherries on a plate

___ ___ ___

$3 \times 4 =$ _____

Groups of Four

Going Further

▶ Using Pictographs

Use the pictograph to answer the questions.

Playground Toys

Soccer balls	☆ ☆ ☆
Jump ropes	☆ ☆ ☆ ☆
Bats	☆ ☆

Key: Each ☆ = 4 toys

1. How many jump ropes are there in all?

    [   ] _____
    label

2. How many more soccer balls are there than bats?

    [   ] _____
    label

3. A school has 8 tennis rackets. How many ☆s are needed to show the tennis rackets in this pictograph?

    [   ] _____
    label

4. **On the Back** How many ☆s are needed to show the soccer balls if each ☆ represents 2 toys? Write the answer and show your work on the back.

Groups of Four

Class Activity

Name _____

Vocabulary

count by
count-bys

▶ **5s Count-Bys**

1. Fill in the chart below to make groups of 5. Then
   count by 5s by saying the last number in each group.

1	2	3	4	5
6	7	8	9	10
	17			
				25
		33		

2. Write out the 5s **count-bys** below.

5 _____ _____ _____ 25 _____ _____ _____ _____ _____

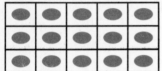

Class Activity

► **Solve Array Problems.**

Write the numbers.

3.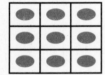

_____ × _____ or

_____ × _____

4.

_____ × _____ or

_____ × _____

5.

_____ × _____

6.

_____ × _____ or

_____ × _____

Plant some beans in your garden.

Your teacher will tell you how.

7.

Groups of Five and Arrays

Name _____

▶ **Use Arrays to Solve Problems**

Here is Mr. and Mrs. Green's orchard.

1. How many apple trees are in the orchard?
   Write the **count-bys** and the **multiplication.**
   Count by 5s.

   _5_   _10_   ____   ____   ____   ____   ____   ____

                       _8_ × _____ = _____

2. Count by 8s.

   _8_   _16_   ____   ____   ____

                       _5_ × _____ = _____

Going Further

Name _____

▶ **Introduce Mystery Multiplication**

You can use an **array** to find the unknown number
in a multiplication sentence.

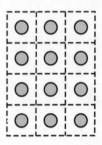

1. How many rows are there in the array? ▢ _____
   label

2. How many columns are there in the array? ▢ _____
   label

3. How many circles are there in all? ▢ _____
   label

4. Complete the multiplication sentence.

   ▢ × 3 = 12

Find the unknown number in each multiplication
sentence. Place beans on the grid to make an array to
help you.

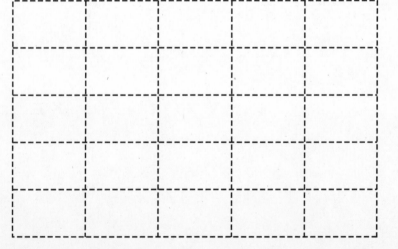

5. 5 × ▢ = 20

6. 4 × ▢ = 8

7. ▢ × 2 = 10

8. ▢ × 3 = 9

Work with Arrays

Class Activity

Name _____

► **Solve and Discuss**

Draw in your answers. Write the numbers.

1. Kathy has **half** as many marbles as Yao.

   Kathy has _____.

   Yao has _____.

Kathy	Yao

2. Paulo and Leah have **equal shares** of blocks.

   Paulo has _____.

   Leah has _____.

Paulo	Leah

3. Nicole has **twice** as many stickers as Reggie.

   Nicole has _____.

   Reggie has _____.

Reggie	Nicole

   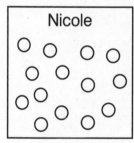

4. Dean has **double** the number of stamps that Yolanda has.

   Yolanda has _____.

   Dean has _____.

   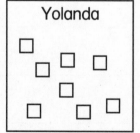

Yolanda	Dean

5. **On the Back** Draw a picture to show equal shares of 14. Explain how you know your picture shows equal shares.

The Language of Shares

Class Activity

Use counters to model each problem.

1. Pedro has 16 cards. How can he share the cards equally with Erik, Dana, and Audrey? Draw a picture.

You can **divide** 16 cards into 4 groups of 4.

2. There are 20 markers. There are 5 friends. How can they share the markers equally?

_____ groups of _____

3. There are 16 marbles in a jar. How can Nick and Warrick share the marbles equally?

_____ groups of _____

4. There are 24 stickers. There are 3 children. How can they share the stickers equally?

_____ groups of _____

5. Use 12 counters. Show different ways you can make equal groups.

13–7

Name _____

Solve. Use **repeated subtraction.**

1. How many times can you subtract 3 from 15?

 The number of times you can subtract 3 is _____.

 $15 \div 3 =$ _____

$15 - 3 =$ _____

_____ $- 3 =$ _____

_____ $- 3 =$ _____

_____ $- 3 =$ _____

_____ $- 3 =$ _____

2. How many times can you subtract 2 from 14?

 The number of times you can subtract 2 is _____.

 $14 \div 2 =$ _____

$14 - 2 =$ _____

_____ $- 2 =$ _____

_____ $- 2 =$ _____

_____ $- 2 =$ _____

_____ $- 2 =$ _____

_____ $- 2 =$ _____

_____ $- 2 =$ _____

3. $9 \div 3 =$ _____ 4. $20 \div 4 =$ _____ 5. $12 \div 3 =$ _____

6. $15 \div 5 =$ _____ 7. $21 \div 3 =$ _____ 8. $18 \div 6 =$ _____

Model Division

Class Activity

Name _____

Vocabulary

symmetrical

▶ Find Lines of Symmetry

Cut out the shapes. Try to fold them in half so that the two parts match exactly. Sort the shapes into two groups: **symmetrical** and not symmetrical.

A

B

C

D

E

F

G

Symmetry

Class Activity

Name _____

► **Complete Drawings of Symmetrical Shapes**

Finish drawing the shapes.

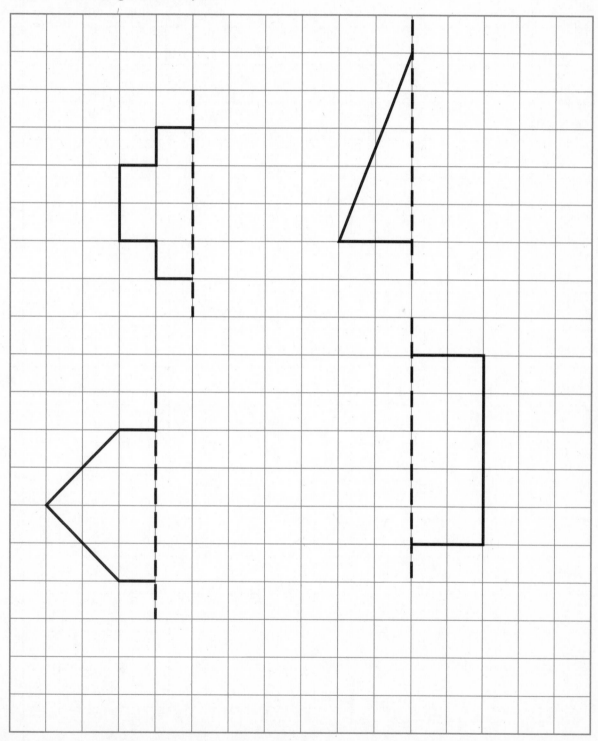

⬦ **On the Back** Draw some symmetrical shapes of your own. Draw a **line of symmetry** for each shape.

Name

Symmetry

Name _____

► Shade Unit Fractions

1. Shade in the fractions for the shapes.

$\frac{1}{2}$

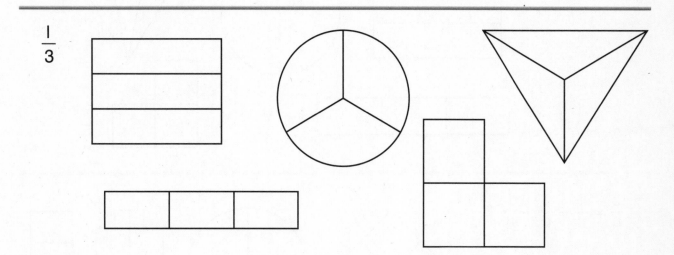

$\frac{1}{3}$

$\frac{1}{4}$

Name _____

Class Activity

▶ **Shade and Write Fractions**

2. Shade in the fractions for the shapes.

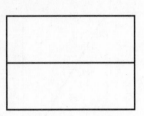

$\frac{1}{2}$

$\frac{2}{3} = \frac{1}{3} + \frac{1}{3}$

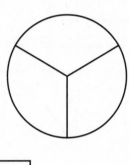
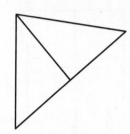

$\frac{3}{4} = \frac{1}{4} + \frac{1}{4} + \frac{1}{4}$

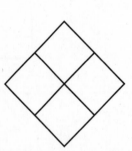
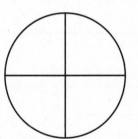
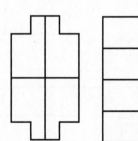

How much is shaded? Write the fraction.

3. 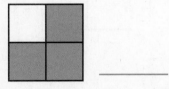 _____

4. 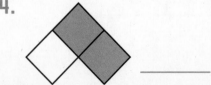 _____

Fractions

Name _____

▶ Divide Shapes Into Equal Parts

Shade in the fractions of the shapes.

$\dfrac{1}{2}$

5.

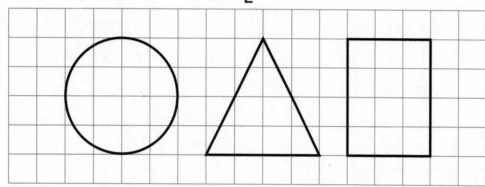

$\dfrac{2}{3} = \dfrac{1}{3} + \dfrac{1}{3}$

6.

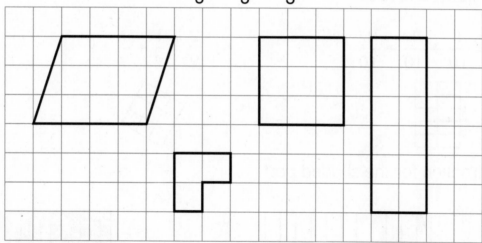

$\dfrac{3}{4} = \dfrac{1}{4} + \dfrac{1}{4} + \dfrac{1}{4}$

7.

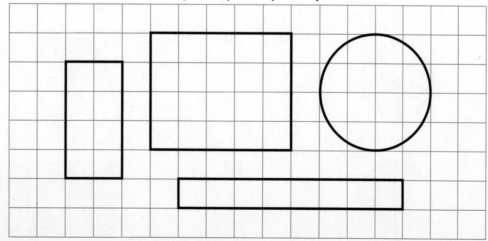

Going Further

► **Solve and Discuss**

Color to show each fraction.

1. $\dfrac{1}{5}$

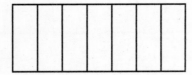

2. $\dfrac{4}{6} = \dfrac{1}{6} + \dfrac{1}{6} + \dfrac{1}{6} + \dfrac{1}{6}$

3. $\dfrac{3}{7} = \dfrac{1}{7} + \dfrac{1}{7} + \dfrac{1}{7}$

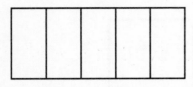

4. $\dfrac{2}{8} = \dfrac{1}{8} + \dfrac{1}{8}$

5. $\dfrac{3}{10} = \dfrac{1}{10} + \dfrac{1}{10} + \dfrac{1}{10}$

6. $\dfrac{2}{9} = \dfrac{1}{9} + \dfrac{1}{9}$

Write the fraction for the shaded part.

7. _____

8. _____

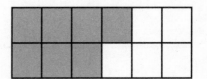

9. _____

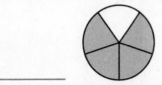

10. _____

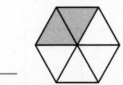

11. _____

12. _____

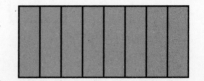

Fractions

Name _____

▶ **Make Fraction Strips**

Color the fraction strips. Cut on the dashed lines.

1. Color 1 whole.	I whole
2. Color $\frac{1}{2}$.	$\frac{1}{2}$ $\frac{1}{2}$
3. Color $\frac{1}{3}$.	$\frac{1}{3}$ $\frac{1}{3}$ $\frac{1}{3}$
4. Color $\frac{2}{3}$. $\frac{2}{3} = \frac{1}{3} + \frac{1}{3}$	$\frac{1}{3}$ $\frac{1}{3}$ $\frac{1}{3}$
5. Color $\frac{1}{4}$.	$\frac{1}{4}$ $\frac{1}{4}$ $\frac{1}{4}$ $\frac{1}{4}$
6. Color $\frac{2}{4}$. $\frac{2}{4} = \frac{1}{4} + \frac{1}{4}$	$\frac{1}{4}$ $\frac{1}{4}$ $\frac{1}{4}$ $\frac{1}{4}$
7. Color $\frac{3}{4}$. $\frac{3}{4} = \frac{1}{4} + \frac{1}{4} + \frac{1}{4}$	$\frac{1}{4}$ $\frac{1}{4}$ $\frac{1}{4}$ $\frac{1}{4}$

More on Fractions

Name _____

Class Activity

▶ **Compare Fractions**

Use your fraction strips to compare the fractions. Then write <, >, or =.

Remember
> means is greater than.
< means is less than.
= means is equal to.

8. Compare $\frac{1}{3}$ and $\frac{1}{2}$.

$\frac{1}{3}$ ◯ $\frac{1}{2}$

9. Compare $\frac{2}{4}$ and $\frac{3}{4}$.

$\frac{2}{4}$ ◯ $\frac{3}{4}$

10. Compare $\frac{2}{3}$ and $\frac{1}{3}$.

$\frac{2}{3}$ ◯ $\frac{1}{3}$

11. Compare $\frac{1}{4}$ and $\frac{1}{2}$.

$\frac{1}{4}$ ◯ $\frac{1}{2}$

12. Compare $\frac{3}{4}$ and $\frac{2}{3}$.

$\frac{3}{4}$ ◯ $\frac{2}{3}$

13. Compare $\frac{2}{3}$ and $\frac{1}{2}$.

$\frac{2}{3}$ ◯ $\frac{1}{2}$

14. Compare $\frac{2}{4}$ and $\frac{1}{2}$.

$\frac{2}{4}$ ◯ $\frac{1}{2}$

15. Compare $\frac{2}{3}$ and $\frac{2}{4}$.

$\frac{2}{3}$ ◯ $\frac{2}{4}$

▶ **Visual Thinking**

Ring the picture that shows the correct amount.

16. less than $\frac{1}{2}$

17. more than $\frac{1}{2}$

13-10

Class Activity

Name _____

▶ Write Money in Different Ways

Complete the chart.

	Money Amount	Number of Cents	Dollars and Cents	Fraction of a Dollar
18.	1 dime	10¢	$0.10	$\frac{1}{10}$
19.	2 dimes	20¢	$0.____	$\frac{}{10}$
20.	3 dimes	____¢	$0.____	$\frac{}{10}$
21.	6 dimes	60¢	$____	$\frac{}{}$
22.	8 dimes	80¢	$____	$\frac{}{}$
23.	10 dimes	____¢	$1.00	$\frac{}{}$ or 1
24.	1 penny	1¢	$0.01	$\frac{1}{100}$
25.	2 pennies	2¢	$____	$\frac{}{100}$
26.	8 pennies	____¢	$____	$\frac{}{100}$
27.	35 pennies	35¢	$____	$\frac{}{100}$
28.	80 pennies	____¢	$0.80	$\frac{}{}$
29.	100 pennies	100¢	$____	$\frac{}{}$ or 1

More on Fractions

▶ Estimate Fractions

Cut on the dashed lines.

0	$\frac{1}{2}$	1

$\frac{1}{2}$	$\frac{1}{2}$

$\frac{1}{3}$	$\frac{1}{3}$	$\frac{1}{3}$

$\frac{1}{4}$	$\frac{1}{4}$	$\frac{1}{4}$	$\frac{1}{4}$

$\frac{1}{5}$	$\frac{1}{5}$	$\frac{1}{5}$	$\frac{1}{5}$	$\frac{1}{5}$

$\frac{1}{6}$	$\frac{1}{6}$	$\frac{1}{6}$	$\frac{1}{6}$	$\frac{1}{6}$	$\frac{1}{6}$

$\frac{1}{7}$	$\frac{1}{7}$	$\frac{1}{7}$	$\frac{1}{7}$	$\frac{1}{7}$	$\frac{1}{7}$	$\frac{1}{7}$

$\frac{1}{8}$	$\frac{1}{8}$	$\frac{1}{8}$	$\frac{1}{8}$	$\frac{1}{8}$	$\frac{1}{8}$	$\frac{1}{8}$	$\frac{1}{8}$

$\frac{1}{9}$	$\frac{1}{9}$	$\frac{1}{9}$	$\frac{1}{9}$	$\frac{1}{9}$	$\frac{1}{9}$	$\frac{1}{9}$	$\frac{1}{9}$	$\frac{1}{9}$

$\frac{1}{10}$	$\frac{1}{10}$	$\frac{1}{10}$	$\frac{1}{10}$	$\frac{1}{10}$	$\frac{1}{10}$	$\frac{1}{10}$	$\frac{1}{10}$	$\frac{1}{10}$	$\frac{1}{10}$

$\frac{1}{11}$	$\frac{1}{11}$	$\frac{1}{11}$	$\frac{1}{11}$	$\frac{1}{11}$	$\frac{1}{11}$	$\frac{1}{11}$	$\frac{1}{11}$	$\frac{1}{11}$	$\frac{1}{11}$	$\frac{1}{11}$

$\frac{1}{12}$	$\frac{1}{12}$	$\frac{1}{12}$	$\frac{1}{12}$	$\frac{1}{12}$	$\frac{1}{12}$	$\frac{1}{12}$	$\frac{1}{12}$	$\frac{1}{12}$	$\frac{1}{12}$	$\frac{1}{12}$	$\frac{1}{12}$

On another piece of paper, write the fractions in order from greatest to least. Then write them from least to greatest. Check children's work.

More on Fractions

Class Activity

Name _____

▶ The Spinner Game

Color the larger part of the spinner blue. 〔 Blue 〕

Color the smaller part of the spinner red. 〔 Red 〕

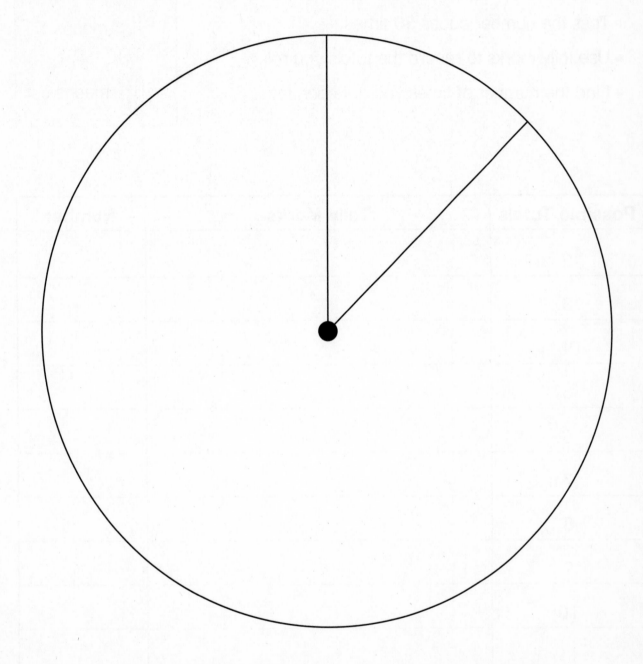

Class Activity

Name _____

Vocabulary

prediction
more likely

▶ **Probability Experiment**

1. Make a **prediction**. Is it **more likely** that you will roll a total of 2 or a total of 7? _____

2. Do the experiment.

  • Toss the number cubes 30 times.

  • Use tally marks to record the totals you roll.

  • Find the number of times you got each total.

Remember

| means 1

卌 means 5

Possible Totals	Tally Marks	Number
2		
3		
4		
5		
6		
7		
8		
9		
10		
11		
12		

Explore Probability

Class Activity

Name _____

▶ **Find All Possible Combinations**

Make an **organized list** to solve the problems.

1. Nadia has a red coat and a blue coat. She also has a yellow hat and a green hat. How many different combinations of a coat and a hat can she wear?

   ☐ different **combinations**

Coat Color		Hat Color
red	→	
red	→	
blue	→	
blue	→	

2. Tia has white, wheat, and rye bread. She also has ham and tuna. How many different kinds of sandwiches can she make?

   ☐ different sandwiches

Bread		Filling
white	→	
white	→	
rye	→	

3. Michael has blue pants and black pants. He also has a red shirt and a green shirt. How many different combinations of pants and shirts can he wear?

   ☐ different combinations

Pants Color		Shirt Color
blue	→	
blue	→	

4. **On the Back** Kara is buying frozen yogurt. She can buy a cone or a cup. She can get vanilla, chocolate, or mint. Make a list of all the different combinations she can buy.

Possible Outcomes

Class Activity

► **Math and Science**

Mr. Miller experiments with plants to see how many flowers bloom. He records data and makes graphs.

This first column in this table shows the number of flowers on three different plants in Week 1.

Number of Flowers on a Plant

Plant	Week 1	Week 2	Week 3
A	2		
B	3		
C	5		

1. In Week 2: Plant A had 3 more flowers than it did in Week 1.
   Plant B had 1 more flower than it did in Week 1.
   Plant C had 3 fewer flowers than it did in Week 1.

   Complete the second column to show the number of flowers on each plant in Week 2.

2. In Week 3, Plant B had 1 more flower than in Week 2, and all three plants had the same number of flowers. Complete the third column to show the number of flowers on each plant in Week 3.

3. Make a bar graph to show the data in the table.

Number of Flowers on a Plant

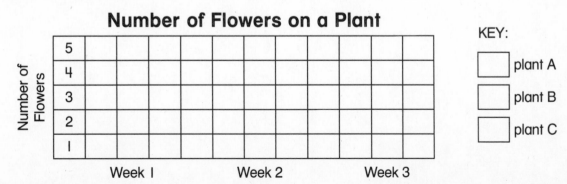

KEY:

☐ plant A

☐ plant B

☐ plant C

Class Activity

▶ **Supporting Math Statements**

Support each statement. Write a paragraph and make a drawing.

1. If there is an even number of objects, equal shares for two people can always be made.

_____

_____

_____

_____

2. If a shape has four sides equal in length and four square corners, the shape is a square.

_____

_____

_____

_____

Use Mathematical Processes

Unit Test

Name _____

1. Count by 2s. Then multiply.
   Shoes

$7 \times 2 =$ _____

___ ___ ___ ___ ___ ___ ___

2. Count by 3s. Then multiply.
   Wheels on a tricycle

$5 \times 3 =$ _____

___ ___ ___ ___ ___

3. Count by 4s. Then multiply.
   Legs on a dog

$6 \times 4 =$ _____

___ ___ ___ ___ ___

4. Count by 5s. Then multiply.
   Fingers on a hand

$8 \times 5 =$ _____

___ ___ ___ ___ ___ ___ ___

Write the numbers.

5.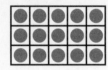

_____ × _____ or

_____ × _____

6.

_____ × _____

7.

_____ × _____ or

_____ × _____

8.

_____ × _____ or

_____ × _____

Draw in your answers. Write the numbers, too.

9. Walt has **twice** as many crayons as Carla.

Carla has _____.

Walt has _____.

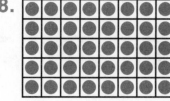

| Carla | Walt |

10. Tony has **half** as many toy cars as Harvey.

Tony has _____.

Harvey has _____.

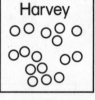

| Tony | Harvey |

Test

Name _____

Draw in your answers. Write the numbers, too.

11. Maria and Rachel have **equal shares** of toys.

    Maria has _____.

    Rachel has _____.

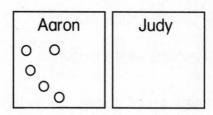

12. Judy has **double** the number of pens that Aaron has.

    Judy has _____.

    Aaron has _____.

Is the figure symmetrical? Write *yes* or *no*.
If yes, draw one line of symmetry.

13.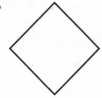

    _____

14.

    _____

15.

    _____

16.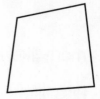

    _____

Write the fraction for the shaded part.

17.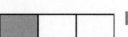

    _____

18.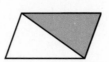

    _____

19.

    _____

20.

    _____

Look at the bag of cubes. Circle the correct event.

21. Which event is certain?

I will pick a black cube.

I will pick a white cube.

22. Which event is impossible?

I will pick a black cube.

I will pick a white cube.

Look at the bag of cubes. How likely are you to pick a 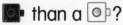 than a 🔲?

23.

more likely

less likely

24.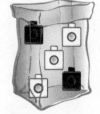

more likely

less likely

25. Extended Response Draw a shape and shade $\frac{3}{4}$ of it.

Class Activity

Name _____

▶ **Non-Standard Units of Length**

1. Find each object. Estimate and then measure the length of each in small and large paper clips.

Object	Estimated length	Measured length
	about _____ about _____	about _____ about _____
	about _____ about _____	about _____ about _____

2. Are the measurement numbers larger with small or large paper clips? Explain.

_____

_____

3. Sona measured the length of a notebook using small paper clips. The length was 35 small paper clips. She then measured the same length using large paper clips. Was her new measurement more than 35 large paper clips? Explain.

_____

_____

14–1

Class Activity

Name _____

Vocabulary

mass

capacity

▶ **Non-Standard Units of Mass**

4. List objects you might use as non-standard units of **mass**.

_____

_____

_____

_____

_____

_____

▶ **Non-Standard Units of Capacity**

5. List objects you might use as non-standard units of **capacity**.

_____

_____

_____

_____

_____

_____

Explore Measurement Concepts

Dear Family,

Your child is beginning another unit on measurement.

Children will first investigate measuring using non-standard units. They will measure length in units such as paper clips and mass in units such as pennies, using a handmade balance scale. Children will arrange containers in order of increasing capacity and test the order by transferring water from one container to another. They will also discuss ideas for measuring volume and time using non-standard units.

Children will continue to measure length in customary units. They will make their own inch ruler and yardstick to measure in inches, feet, and yards. They will also make conversions between customary units using these relationships:

1 foot = 12 inches
1 yard = 3 feet
1 yard = 36 inches

These are examples of the types of conversion they will do for homework in Lesson 2.

1 ft = _____12_____ in.   3 ft = _____36_____ in.   2 yd = _____6_____ ft

In the last lesson of this unit, children will have an opportunity to measure length, mass, weight, capacity, time, and temperature using standard units.

To help bridge your child's classroom learning with home, ask your child to estimate and measure objects that he or she uses in everyday activities. For example, you might ask, "How much do you think this pot holds?" and have your child measure its capacity in cups.

If you have any questions or comments, please call or write to me.

Sincerely,
Your child's teacher

Estimada familia:

Su niño empieza otra unidad sobre las medidas.

Los niños empezarán a medir con unidades no usuales. Medirán la longitud usando sujetapapeles y la masa usando unidades tales como monedas de un centavo con una balanza que ellos harán. Los niños ordenarán recipientes según su capacidad y comprobarán el orden pasando agua de un recipiente a otro. También comentarán ideas para medir el volumen y el tiempo usando unidades no usuales.

Más adelante, los niños medirán la longitud en unidades del sistema usual. Harán su propia regla de pulgadas y su propia regla de 1 yarda para medir en pulgadas, pies y yardas. También harán conversiones entre estas unidades utilizando las siguientes relaciones:

1 pie = 12 pulgadas
1 yarda = 3 pies
1 yarda = 36 pulgadas

Estos son ejemplos de los tipos de conversiones que harán como tarea para la Lección 2.

1 pie = _____12_____ pulg   3 pies = _____36_____ pulg

2 yd = _____6_____ pies

En la última lección de esta unidad los niños tendrán la oportunidad de medir la longitud, la masa, el peso, la capacidad, el tiempo y la temperatura usando unidades usuales de medida.

Para ayudar a su niño a hacer la conexión entre el aprendizaje en la escuela y la casa, pídale que estime y mida objetos que se usan en las actividades diarias. Por ejemplo, podría preguntarle, "¿Cuánto crees que cabe en esta olla?" y pedirle que mida su capacidad usando una taza.

Si tiene alguna duda o comentario, por favor comuníquese conmigo.

Atentamente,
El maestro de su niño

Explore Measurement Concepts

► Make an Inch Ruler

Directions:

Step 1: Cut along the dashed lines.

Step 2: Place the sections in the correct order.

Step 3: Tape or glue together the sections at the tab.

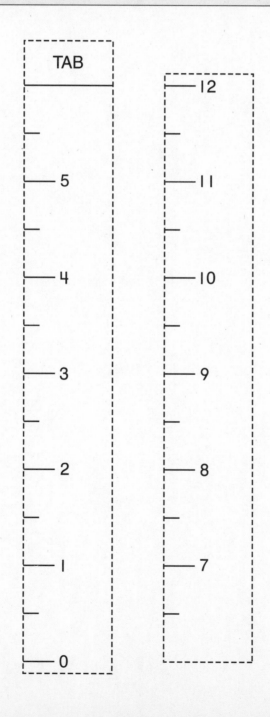

Inch Ruler

Class Activity

► **Measure to the Nearest Inch**

To measure to the nearest **inch (in.)**, place the zero mark on your ruler at the left end of the object. Find the inch mark that is closest to the right end of the object.

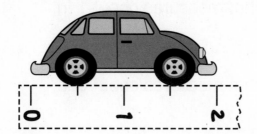

To the nearest inch, the length of this toy car is 2 inches.

Measure the length of each object to the nearest inch.

1. 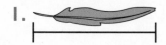 _____

2. 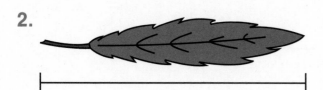 _____

3.  _____

4. Draw a horizontal line that is 2 in. long.

5. Draw a horizontal line that is 6 in. long.

Name _____

Class Activity

▶ **Estimate and Measure in Inches**

6. Describe a part of your hand that measures about 2 in.

   _____

7. Describe a part of your hand that measures about I in.

   _____

8. Describe a part of your hand that measures about 6 in.

   _____

Estimate and measure the length of each line segment.

9. ▬▬▬▬▬▬▬▬▬▬▬▬▬▬▬

   Estimated length: _____

   Measured length: _____

10. ▬▬▬▬▬▬▬▬▬▬▬▬▬▬▬▬▬▬

   Estimated length: _____

   Measured length: _____

11. Find four classroom objects that you can measure in
    inches. Estimate and then measure the length of
    each object to the nearest inch. Complete the table.

Object	Estimated length (in.)	Measured length (in.)

Class Activity

► **Make a Yardstick**

Directions:

> **Step 1:** Cut along the dashed lines.
>
> **Step 2:** Place the sections in the correct order.
>
> **Step 3:** Tape or glue together the sections at the tab.

TAB	TAB	TAB	TAB	TAB	
					36
5	11	17	23	29	35
4	10	16	22	28	34
3	9	15	21	27	33
2	8	14	20	26	32
1	7	13	19	25	31
0					

Yardstick

Class Activity

Name _____

Vocabulary
foot (ft)
yard (yd)

▶ Measure in Feet and Yards

Find each length to the nearest **foot (ft).**

12. width of your desk

13. length from your knee to your ankle

_____

Find each length to the nearest **yard (yd).**

14. height of the classroom door

15. length of a bookshelf

_____

Measure each length to the nearest foot and to the nearest yard.

16. width of the classroom door

17. length of the classroom board

_____ ft

_____ ft

_____ yd

_____ yd

18. What do you notice about the numbers when you measure in yards instead of feet?

_____

▶ Select a Unit

Tell the unit you would use to measure the length of each object. Write _inch_, _foot_, or _yard_.

19.

_____

20.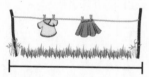

_____

21.

_____

22.

_____

Class Activity

Name _____

► **Change Units**

Customary Units of Length
1 ft = 12 in.
1 yd = 3 ft
1 yd = 36 in.

Complete each table.

23.

Feet	1	2	3	4	5	6
Inches	12	24				

24.

Yards	1	2	3	4	5	6
Feet	3	6				

25.

Yards	1	2	3	4	5	6
Inches	36	72				

26. Fill in the correct number.

2 ft = _____ in.   1 yd = _____ ft   24 in. = _____ ft

4 yd = _____ ft   36 in. = _____ ft   5 ft = _____ in.

Customary Units of Length

Class Activity

Vocabulary
cup
pint
quart
gallon

Use **cup**, **pint**, **quart**, and **gallon** containers to answer each question.

1. How many cups fit in a pint? _____

2. How many cups fit in a quart? _____

3. How many cups fit in a gallon? _____

4. How many pints fit in a quart? _____

5. How many pints fit in a gallon? _____

6. How many quarts fit in a gallon? _____

Find how many of each fill containers A and B.

7.

Container	Number of Cups	Number of Pints	Number of Quarts
A			
B			

Class Activity

Vocabulary

ounce

pound

Find classroom objects that weigh about an **ounce.**

Weigh them. Fill in the chart.

1.

Less than 1 Ounce	About 1 Ounce	More than 1 Ounce

Find classroom objects that weigh about a **pound.**

Weigh them. Fill in the chart.

2.

Less than 1 Pound	About 1 Pound	More than 1 Pound

Measurement

Unit Test

Measure the length of each object to the nearest inch.

1.

_____

2.

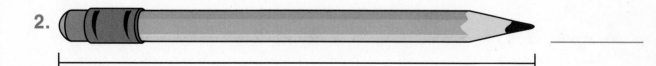

_____

3.

_____

Fill in the correct number.

4. I yd = _____ in.

5. I ft = _____ in.

6. I yd = _____ ft

7. 24 in. = _____ ft

8. 9 ft = _____ yd

9. 72 in. = _____ yd

10. **Extended Response** If you measured the length of the classroom board in inches and in yards, which measure would have a larger number? Explain.

_____

_____

_____

_____

_____

Name _____

Write the value of each set using a **cent sign**.
Then ring the set with the greater value.

1.

_____   _____

2.

_____   _____

3.

_____   _____

Order the coin sets from **least** to **greatest**.

4.

_____   _____   _____

Class Activity

Name _____

Write the value of each set using a **dollar sign** and **dollar notation**.
Then ring the set with the greater value.

1.

_____   _____

2.

_____   _____

3.

_____   _____

4.

_____   _____

Class Activity

Use the 120 Poster.

Skip count forward and backward.

1. Start at 3. Skip count forward by 5s.
   Color each box green.

2. Start at 100. Skip count backward by 5s.
   Color each box blue.

3. Start at 119. Skip count backward by 5s.
   Color each box brown.

4. What pattern do you see for skip-counting by 5s?

   _____

   _____

5. Start at 8. Skip count forward by 10s.
   Color each box yellow.

6. Start at 100. Skip count backward by 10s.
   Circle each box.

7. Start at 92. Skip count backward by 10s.
   Color each box orange.

8. Start at 6. Skip count forward by 10s.
   Color each box red.

9. What pattern do you see for skip-counting by 10s?

   _____

   _____

Class Activity

Name _____

Use a calculator to skip count.

Write each number after you enter the equal sign.

1. Start at 4. Skip count forward by 10s.

   Enter ④ then ⊕ ① ⓪ ⊜ . Then continue entering ⊜ .

   4, _____, _____, _____, _____, _____, _____, _____, _____, _____

2. Start at 29. Skip count forward by 10s.

   29, _____, _____, _____, _____, _____, _____, _____, _____, _____

3. Start at 91. Skip count backward by 10s.

   91, _____, _____, _____, _____, _____, _____, _____, _____, _____

4. Start at 127. Skip count backward by 10s.

   127, _____, _____, _____, _____, _____, _____, _____, _____, _____

5. Start at 4. Skip count forward by 5s.

   4, _____, _____, _____, _____, _____, _____, _____, _____, _____

6. Start at 27. Skip count forward by 5s.

   27, _____, _____, _____, _____, _____, _____, _____, _____, _____

7. Start at 86. Skip count backward by 5s.

   86, _____, _____, _____, _____, _____, _____, _____, _____, _____

8. Start at 63. Skip count backward by 5s.

   63, _____, _____, _____, _____, _____, _____, _____, _____, _____

Count Different Ways

Class Activity

Name _____

Use the **line graph** to answer the questions.

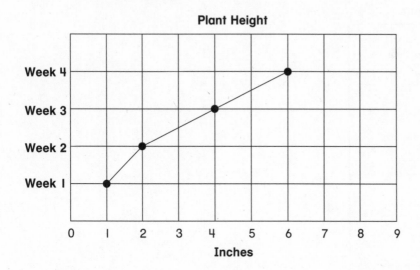

Plant Height

1. What is the title of the graph? _____

2. How much time does this graph represent?

_____

3. What change is happening over the weeks?

_____

4. How much did the plant grow between
Week 1 and Week 2? _____

5. How much did the plant grow between
Week 2 and Week 3? _____

6. How much did the plant grow between
Week 3 and Week 4? _____

7. How much did the plant grow between
Week 1 and Week 4? _____

Class Activity

Use the line graph to answer the questions.

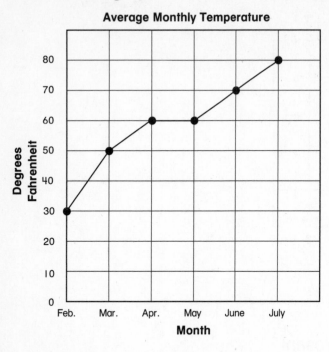

Average Monthly Temperature

1. What is the title of the graph? _____

2. How much time does this graph represent?

   _____

3. What change is happening over the months?

   _____

4. How much did the temperature rise between February and March? _____

5. How much did the temperature rise between March and April? _____

6. How much did the temperature rise between May and June? _____

7. Between which two months did the temperature stay the same? _____

8. Between which two months did the temperature rise the most? _____

Class Activity

Name _____

Use the **three-dimensional shapes** to predict and build new shapes.

1. Predict what shape you can make by combining a cube and a pyramid. Then combine the 2 shapes and draw the shape they make.

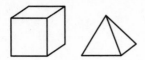

2. Predict what shape you can make by combining a rectangular prism and a cylinder. Then combine the 2 shapes and draw the shape they make.

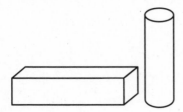

3. Predict what shape you can make by combining a cylinder, a rectangular prism, and a pyramid. Then combine the 3 shapes and draw the shape they make.

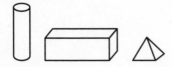

Class Activity

Use clay to make the named shape.
Then predict and cut apart the shape to make new shapes.

1. Predict what shapes you will make by cutting apart a cube.
   Then cut the shape and draw the new shapes.

2. Predict what shapes you will make by cutting apart a sphere.
   Then cut the shape and draw the new shapes.

3. Predict what shapes you will make by cutting apart a pyramid.
   Then cut the shape and draw the new shapes.

Explore 3-Dimensional Shapes

Glossary

A

add

••••   ••
 4 + 2 = 6

addend

5 + 6 = 11
↑   ↑
addends

Adding Up Method (for Subtraction)

144
− 68
76

68 + 2 = 70
70 + 30 = 100
100 + 44 = 144

76

after

98, 99

99 is after 98.

A.M.

The hours between midnight and noon.

angle

These are angles.

area

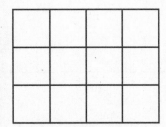

Area = 12 square units

You can find the area of a figure by covering it with square units and counting them.

array

This picture shows a 3 × 5 or 5 × 3 array.

B

bar graph

Coins in My Collection

horizontal bar graph

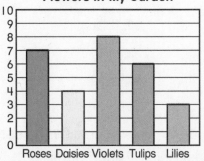

Flowers in My Garden

vertical bar graph

Glossary (Continued)

before

$31, 32$

31 is before 32.

between

$81, 82, 83$

82 is between 81 and 83.

break-apart

You can break apart a larger number to get two smaller amounts called break-aparts.

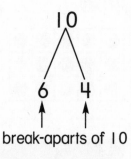

break-aparts of 10

C

calendar

March						
February						
January						
Sun	Mon	Tues	Wed	Thurs	Fri	Sat
1	2	3	4	5	6	7
8	9	10	11	12	13	14
15	16	17	18	19	20	21
22	23	24	25	26	27	28
29	30	31				

capacity

Capacity is how much a container holds. This container holds 1 quart of milk.

cent

front   back

1 cent or 1¢ or $0.01

centimeter (cm)

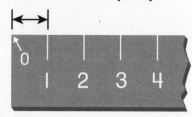

certain

You are certain to choose a black button from the jar.

change minus problem

Sarah had 12 books.
Then she loaned her friend 9 books.
How many books does Sarah have now?

$$12 - 9 = \boxed{3}$$

had   loaned   now

Any number may be unknown.

change plus problem

Alvin had 9 toy cars.
Then he got 3 more.
How many toy cars does he have now?

$$9 + 3 = \boxed{12}$$

had   got   now

Any number may be unknown.

collection problem

Jason put 8 large plates and 4 small plates on the table. How many plates are on the table altogether?

$$8 + 4 = \boxed{12}$$

large   small   altogether

Any number may be unknown.

circle graph

Animals at Grasslands Nature Park

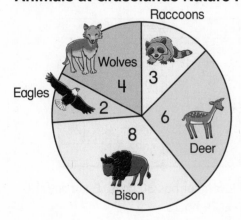

Raccoons

Wolves
4

3

Eagles

2

8

6

Deer

Bison

comparison problem

Joe has 6 roses. Sasha has 9 roses. How many more roses does Sasha have than Joe?

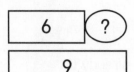

6   ?

9

J   S
$$6 + \square = 9$$
$$9 - 6 = \boxed{3}$$
S   J

cone

clock

analog clock

digital clock

congruent

These are congruent figures.   These are not congruent figures.

Congruent figures have the same size and shape.

Glossary (Continued)

count all

$$5 + 3 = \square$$

1 2 3 4 5 | 6 7 8

● ● ● ● ● | ● ● ●

$$5 + 3 = \boxed{8}$$

count by/count-bys

I can count by 2s.

2, 4, 6, 8, 10, 12, 14, 16, 18, and 20 are 2s count-bys.

count on

$$5 + 3 = \boxed{8}$$

$$5 + \boxed{3} = 8$$

$$8 - 5 = \boxed{3}$$

Already 5

cube

cylinder

D

data

	Hamsters	Mice
Kendra	5	8
Scott	2	9
Ida	7	3

data

The data in the table show how many hamsters and how many mice each child has.

day

November						
Sun	Mon	Tues	Wed	Thurs	Fri	Sat
	1	2	3	4	5	6
7	8	9	10	11	12	13
14	15	16	17	18	19	20
21	22	23	24	25	26	27
28	39	30				

November has 30 days. Each day has 24 hours.

decade numbers

10, 20, 30, 40, 50, 60, 70, 80, 90

decade partners

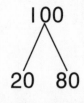

20 and 80 are decade partners of 100.

decimal point

$4.25

↑
decimal point

decimeter (dm)

decimeter

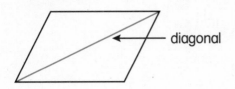

10 centimeters = 1 decimeter
(not drawn to scale)

denominator

$$\frac{3}{4} \longleftarrow \text{denominator}$$

The number of equal parts into which the 1 whole is divided.

diagonal

diagonal

difference

$$11 - 3 = 8$$

$$\begin{array}{r} 11 \\ - 3 \\ \hline \text{difference} \longrightarrow 8 \end{array}$$

digits

0, 1, 2, 3, 4, 5, 6, 7, 8, 9

dime

front   back

10 cents or 10¢ or $0.10

divide

$$15 \div 3 = 5$$

dollar

100 cents or

100¢ or $1.00

   front

   back

dollar sign

$4.25

↑

dollar sign

doubles

Both addends (or partners) are the same.

$$4 + 4 = 8$$

doubles minus 1

7 + 7 = 14, so

7 + 6 = 13, 1 less than 14.

doubles plus 1

6 + 6 = 12, so

6 + 7 = 13, 1 more than 12.

Glossary (Continued)

edge

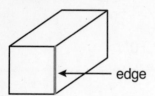

edge

equal shares

Maria

Rachel

Maria and Rachel have equal shares of pennies.

equal to

5 + 3 = 8

5 plus 3 is equal to 8.

equation

$4 + 3 = 7$ $7 = 4 + 3$

$9 - 5 = 4$ $4 + 5 = 8 + 1$

An equation must have an = sign.

equation chain

$3 + 4 = 5 + 2 = 8 - 1 = 7$

estimate

An estimate is a number that is close to an exact amount.

$$\begin{array}{r} 28 \\ + 23 \\ \hline \end{array} \longrightarrow \begin{array}{r} 30 \\ + 20 \\ \hline 50 \end{array}$$ You can estimate a sum.

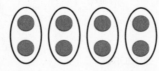 about 10   You can estimate the number of objects in a set.

even number

A number is even if you can make groups of 2 and have none left over.

8 is an even number.

exact change

43¢

I will pay with 4 dimes and 3 pennies. That is the exact change. I won't get any money back.

Expanded Method (for Addition)

$$\begin{array}{r} 78 = 70 + 8 \\ + 57 = 50 + 7 \\ \hline 120 + 15 = 135 \end{array}$$

Expanded Method (for Subtraction)

$$64 = \cancel{60}^{50} + \cancel{4}^{+14}$$
$$- 28 = 20 + 8$$
$$\overline{ 30 + 6 = 36}$$

expanded number

$$283 = 200 + 80 + 3$$

F

face

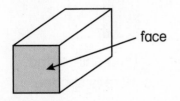

face

fair shares

fewer

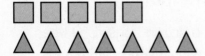

There are fewer ◻ than △ .

flip

You can **flip** a figure over a **horizontal line**.

You can **flip** a figure over a **vertical line**.

foot (ft)

foot

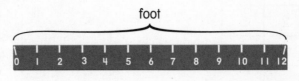

12 inches = 1 foot   (not drawn to scale)

fourth

 1 whole

 $\frac{1}{4}$

$\frac{1}{4}$ (one fourth) of the square is shaded.

fraction

4 equal parts $\frac{3}{4}$ is 3 out of 4 equal parts.

$$\frac{3}{4} = \frac{1}{4} + \frac{1}{4} + \frac{1}{4}$$

The fraction of the square that is shaded is $\frac{3}{4}$.

Glossary (Continued)

front-end estimation

$$
\begin{array}{rcr}
\underline{\scriptstyle ③}4 & \longrightarrow & 30 \\
+\,\underline{\scriptstyle ①}5 & \longrightarrow & +\ 10 \\
\hline
 & & 40
\end{array}
$$

function table

Add 3.	
0	3
1	4
2	5
3	6

G

greater than

$$34 \quad > \quad 25$$

34 is greater than 25.

greatest

25   41   63

63 is the greatest number.

group name

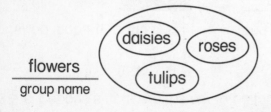

flowers
group name

growing pattern

A number or geometric pattern that increases.

Examples: 2, 4, 6, 8, 10...

1, 2, 5, 10, 17...

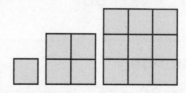

H

half

I whole

$\frac{1}{2}$

$\frac{1}{2}$ (one half) of the square is shaded.

half-hour

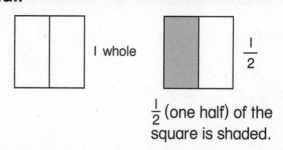

5 minutes
10 minutes
15 minutes
20 minutes
25 minutes
30 minutes

30 minutes = 1 half-hour

hidden information

Heather bought a dozen eggs. She used 7 of them to make breakfast. How many eggs does she have left?

$12 - 7 = \boxed{5}$

The hidden information is that a dozen means 12.

horizontal

$$4 + 5 = 9$$

horizontal form

horizontal line

hour

60 minutes = 1 hour

hour hand

hour hand

hundreds

3 hundreds

347 has 3 hundreds.

↑

hundreds

impossible

It is impossible to choose a white button from this jar.

inch (in.)

1 inch

key

Apples Bought

Red	🍎 🍎 🍎 🍎
Green	🍎 🍎
Yellow	🍎 🍎

Key: Each 🍎 stands for 2 apples.

least

14   7   63

7 is the least number.

length

The length of the pencil is about 17 cm.

Glossary (Continued)

less likely

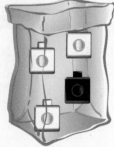

It is less likely that I will choose a black cube than a white cube if I choose a cube without looking.

less than

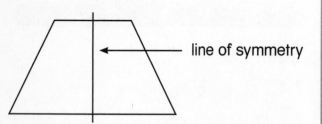

45 is less than 46.

line

line of symmetry

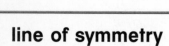

line segment

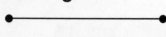

Make a Ten

$8 + 6 = \boxed{}$

$8 \bullet\bullet | \bullet\bullet\bullet\bullet$

$10 + 4$

$10 + 4 = 14,$

so $8 + 6 = 14$

make change

Sellers make change when they give back money when a buyer pays too much.

mass

You can use a balance scale to compare mass.

matching drawing

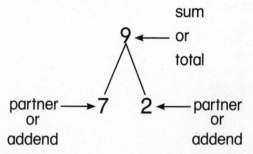

Math Mountain

measure

You measure to find the length, weight, mass, capacity, volume, or temperature of an object. You find how many units.

meter(m)

100 centimeters = 1 meter
(not drawn to scale)

midpoint

midpoint

The point exactly halfway between the ends of a line segment is the midpoint.

minus

8 − 3 = 5

$$\begin{array}{r} 8 \\ -\ 3 \\ \hline 5 \end{array}$$

8 minus 3 equals 5.

minute

I minute

60 seconds = 1 minute

minute hand

minute hand: points to the minutes

money string

$1.00 = 25¢ + 25¢ + 25¢ + 10¢ + 10¢ + 5¢

month

June						
Sun	Mon	Tues	Wed	Thurs	Fri	Sat
				1	2	3
4	5	6	7	8	9	10
11	12	13	14	15	16	17
18	19	20	21	22	23	24
25	26	27	28	29	30	

June is the sixth month. There are twelve months in a year.

more

○ ○ ○ ○ ○ ○ ○
▢ ▢ ▢ ▢ ▢

There are more ○ than ▢.

more likely

It is more likely that I will choose a black button than a white button if I choose a button without looking.

Glossary (Continued)

multiply

$3 \times 5 = 15$

$5 + 5 + 5$

3 fives

not equal to

$6 + 4 \neq 8$

$6 + 4$ is not equal to 8.

New Groups Above Method

$$\begin{array}{r} \overset{1}{5}6 \\ + 28 \\ \hline 84 \end{array}$$

$6 + 8 = 14$

The 1 new ten in 14 goes up to the tens place.

number line

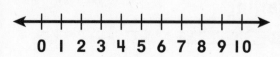

This is a number line.

New Groups Below Method

$$\begin{array}{r} 56 \\ + 2\underset{1}{8} \\ \hline 84 \end{array}$$

$6 + 8 = 14$

The 1 new ten in 14 goes below in the tens place.

number path

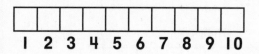

This is a number path.

nickel

front   back

5 cents or 5¢ or $0.05

numerator

$\dfrac{3}{4}$ ← numerator

$\dfrac{3}{4} = \dfrac{1}{4} + \dfrac{1}{4} + \dfrac{1}{4}$

The numerator tells how many unit fractions.

non-standard unit

The length of the pencil is 5 paper clips.

A paper clip is a non-standard unit of length. An inch and a centimeter are standard units of length.

odd number

A number is odd if you can make groups of 2 and have one left over.

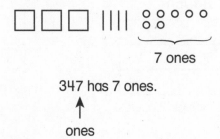

9 is an odd number.

ones

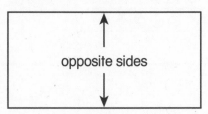

7 ones

347 has 7 ones.

↑

ones

opposite sides

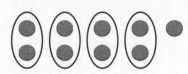

opposite sides

order

2, 5, 6

The numbers 2, 5, and 6 are in order from least to greatest.

ordinal number

Ordinal numbers name positions.

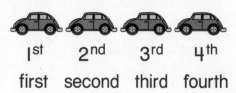

1st   2nd   3rd   4th

first   second   third   fourth

parallel

Lines or line segments that are always the same distance apart.

parallelogram

A parallelogram has 2 pairs of parallel sides.

Partner House

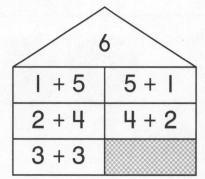

Glossary (Continued)

partner lengths

partner lengths of 4 cm

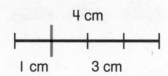

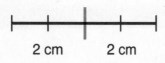

partners

$9 + 6 = 15$

partners

addends

pattern

2, 4, 6, 8, 10, 12

These are patterns.

penny

front   back

1 cent or 1¢ or $0.01

perimeter

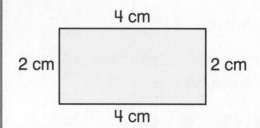

perimeter = 2 cm + 4 cm + 2 cm + 4 cm = 12 cm
Perimeter is the total length of the sides.

pictograph

Apples Bought

Red	🍎 🍎 🍎 🍎
Green	🍎 🍎
Yellow	🍎 🍎

Key: Each 🍎 stands for 2 apples.

picture graph

Flowers	🌸 🌸 🌸 🌸 🌸 🌸
Vases	🏺 🏺 🏺 🏺 🏺 🏺 🏺 🏺

pie graph

Animals at Grasslands Nature Park

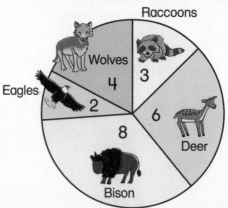

same as a circle graph

plus

$3 + 2 = 5$

3 plus 2 equals 5.

$$\begin{array}{r} 3 \\ + 2 \\ \hline 5 \end{array}$$

P.M.

The hours between noon and midnight.

polygons

Polygons have sides that are line segments.

possible

It is possible to choose a white button.

It is possible to choose a black button.

predict

I think it will rain tomorrow.

I predict that it will rain tomorrow.

probability

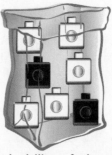

· What is the probability of choosing a white cube?

· It is likely.

proof drawing

Proof Drawing

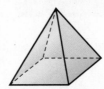

$86 + 57 = 143$

pyramids

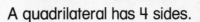
Q

quadrilateral

A quadrilateral has 4 sides.

Glossary (Continued)

quarter

front   back

25 cents or 25¢ or $0.25

Quick Hundreds

347

Quick Hundreds

Quick Tens

162

Quick Tens

rectangle

A rectangle has 4 sides and
4 right angles.

rectangular prism

regular polygons

A regular polygon has all sides and all
angles equal.

repeating pattern

A pattern consisting of a group of numbers,
letters, or figures that repeat.

Examples: 1, 2, 1, 2, ...

        A, B, C, A, B, C, ...

right angle

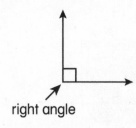

right angle

rotation

You can **turn** or **rotate** a figure around a point.

round

44 is closer to 40 than 50.
44 rounds to 40.

ruler

A ruler is used to measure length.

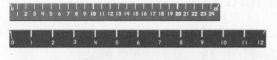

scale

Coins in My Collection

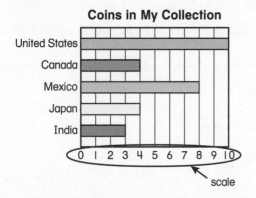

The numbers along the side or the bottom of a graph.

sequence

Sequences follow a pattern.

2, 4, 6, . . .

9, 8, 7, . . .

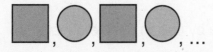

Show All Totals Method

```
  25        724
+ 48      + 158
  60         12
  13         70
  73        800
            882
```

similar

These figures are similar. These figures are similar. These figures are not similar.

Similar figures always have the same shape and sometimes have the same size.

situation equation

A baker baked 100 loaves of bread. He sold some loaves. There are 73 loaves left. How many loaves of bread did he sell?

$$100 - \boxed{} = 73$$

situation equation

skip count

skip count by 2s: 2, 4, 6, 8, . . .
skip count by 5s: 5, 10, 15, 20, . . .

Glossary (Continued)

slide

You can **slide** a figure right or left along a straight line.

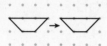

You can slide a figure up or down along a straight line.

solution equation

A baker baked 100 loaves of bread. He sold some loaves. There are 73 loaves left. How many loaves of bread did he sell?

$100 - 73 = \boxed{}$

$\underbrace{}$
solution equation

sphere

square

A square has 4 equal sides and 4 right angles.

square centimeter

Each side measures
1 centimeter.

1 square centimeter

square unit

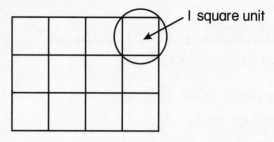

I square unit

The area of this rectangle is 12 square units.

standard unit

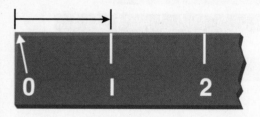

An inch is a standard unit of length.
A paper clip is a non-standard unit of length.

subtract

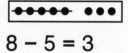

$8 - 5 = 3$

sum

$4 + 3 = 7$

sum

$$\begin{array}{r} 4 \\ + 3 \\ \hline 7 \end{array}$$

sum ⟶

survey

To collect data by asking people questions.

switch the partners

Show partners in a different order.

$$6 + 4 = 10 \qquad 4 + 6 = 10$$

↑ ↑   ↑ ↑

partners   partners

The total is the same.

symmetry

A figure has symmetry if it can be folded along a line so that the two halves match exactly.

table

	Hamsters	Mice
Kendra	5	8
Scott	2	9
Ida	7	3

tally chart

Favorite Color	Tally Marks	Number of Students
red	||||	4
blue	⊬||| |	6
yellow	⊬||| ||	7

teen number

any number from 11 to 19

11 12 13 14 15 16 17 18 19

temperature

A thermometer measures the temperature.

tens

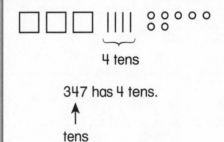

4 tens

347 has 4 tens.

↑

tens

third

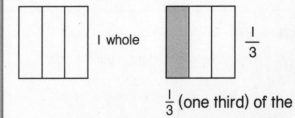

1 whole

$\frac{1}{3}$

$\frac{1}{3}$ (one third) of the square is shaded.

Glossary (Continued)

thousand

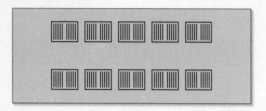

1,000 = ten hundreds

time

			January			
Sun	Mon	Tues	Wed	Thurs	Fri	Sat
1	2	3	4	5	6	7
8	9	10	11	12	13	14
15	16	17	18	19	20	21
22	23	24	25	26	27	28
29	30	31				

Time is measured in hours, minutes, seconds, days, weeks, months, and years.

total

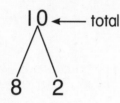

10 ← total

8   2

triangle

A triangle has 3 sides.

turn

You can **turn** or **rotate** a figure around a point.

twice

Jeremy

Michael

Jeremy has twice as many books as Michael.

U

ungroup

$$\begin{array}{r} 0\ \overset{2}{\cancel{3}}\ \overset{14}{\cancel{4}} \\ \cancel{1}\cancel{3}\cancel{4} \\ -\ \ 78 \\ \hline 56 \end{array}$$

Ungroup when you need more ones or tens to subtract.

Ungroup First Method

$$\begin{array}{r} 64 \\ -28 \\ \hline \uparrow\ \ \uparrow \end{array}$$
yes no

1. Check to see if there are enough tens and ones to subtract.

$$\begin{array}{r} \overset{5}{\cancel{6}}\ \overset{14}{\cancel{4}} \\ -\ 28 \end{array}$$

2. You can get more ones by taking from the tens and putting them in the ones place.

$$\begin{array}{r} \overset{5}{\cancel{6}}\ \overset{14}{\cancel{4}} \\ -\ 28 \\ \hline 36 \end{array}$$

3. Subtract from either right to left or left to right.

unknown

$$3 + \boxed{} = 9$$
↑
unknown partner

$$3 + 6 = \boxed{}$$
↑
unknown total

V

Venn diagram

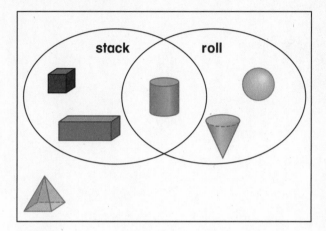

vertex

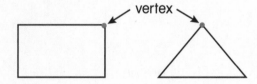

vertex

vertical

$$\begin{array}{r} 4 \\ + 3 \\ \hline 7 \end{array}$$

vertical form   vertical line

view

This is the side view of the rectangular prism above.

volume

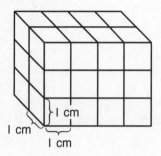

1 cm
1 cm
1 cm

The volume of this rectangular prism is 24 cubic centimeters.

W

weight

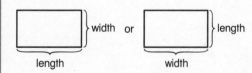

2 lb

The weight of this book is 2 pounds.

width

width or length

length   width

Glossary (Continued)

word name

12

twelve ◄——— word name

Y

yard (yd)

3 feet = 1 yard (not drawn to scale)